Study Guide
to

Six Classic Sherlock Holmes Stories

by Sir Arthur Conan Doyle

by Ray Moore M.A.

Acknowledgements:

As always, I am indebted to the work of numerous critics and reviewers. Where I am conscious of having taken an idea or a phrase from a particular author, I have cited the source in the text. Any failure to do so is an omission which I will immediately correct if it is drawn to my attention. Brief quotations from such sources are made to support the writer's analysis. To the best of my knowledge, this constitutes 'fair use'.

The text of the Conan Doyle stories included here is in the public domain. A 2014 court ruling found that all of the Sherlock Holmes short stories were free from copyright with the exception of the last ten stories Doyle wrote which are to remain under copyright protection until 2022-23. None of those stories is included in this volume.

The two illustrations by Sidney Paget used are. They are likewise in the public domain.

Thanks are due to my wife, Barbara, for reading the manuscript, for offering valuable suggestions, and for putting the text into the correct formats for publication. Any errors which remain are my own.

Copyright

First Edition June 2019
Copyright © 2019 Ray Moore
All rights reserved.

Sherlock Holmes (1904) by Sidney Paget (1860-1908).

Contents

The Detective Story: An Introduction 1
    The Detective Story: Birth of a Genre 1
    Elements of the Classic Detective Mystery: 5
    The Sherlock Holmes Canon 8
    Introducing Holmes and Watson 12

The Red-Headed League 17
    Structure of the Story: 17
    The Detective's Methods: 18
    Holmes and the Regular Police: 20
    Be a detective... "The Red headed League" 22

The Man with The Twisted Lip 27
    Structure of the Story: 27
    The Detective's Methods: 28
    Holmes and the Regular Police: 29
    Be a detective..."The Man with the Twisted Lip" 30

The Speckled Band 35
    The Structure of the Story: 35
    The Detective's Methods: 36
    Holmes and the Regular Police: 37
    Be a detective... "The Speckled Band" 39
    Sherlock Holmes' Copy of the Will of Mrs. Roylott 43

Silver Blaze 47
    The Structure of the Story: 47
    The Detective's Methods: 48
    Holmes and the Regular Police: 50
    Be a detective... "Silver Blaze" 51

The Cardboard Box 55
    The Structure of the Story: 55
    The Detective's Methods: 56
    Holmes and the Regular Police: 57
    Be a detective... "The Cardboard Box" 58

The Final Problem **61**
   Introduction to "The Final Problem" 61
   Structure of the Story: 61
   The Detective's Methods: 62
   Holmes and the Regular Police: 62
   Be a detective: The Death of Sherlock Holmes 63
   Sherlock Holmes explains his escape to Dr. Watson 66

Reading Group Use of the Study Guide Questions **70**

The Reverend Lyle Thorne Mysteries **72**

About the Author **75**

Sherlock Holmes Short Stories by Sir Arthur Conan Doyle

The Detective Story: An Introduction

The Detective Story: Birth of a Genre

The detective story is so popular today that, without thinking about it, we tend to assume that the genre has always been around. Surprisingly, detective mysteries are (with one controversial exception) a relatively modern literary innovation dating back only to the middle of the nineteenth century.

In some ways, the first detective mystery in world literature is the Classical Greek tragedy *Oedipus Rex* by Sophocles which was first performed circa 429 BC. Oedipus, King of Thebes, is informed by the Oracle at Delphi that the plague which is ravaging his city will only end when the murderer of the previous king, Laius, is discovered and brought to justice. Oedipus (the first detective in the first 'Whodunit?') conducts a thorough enquiry by questioning all of the witnesses still living and assembling the evidence. This logical approach points unerringly to Oedipus himself as the murderer and the process uncovers even more terrible truths about Oedipus' past. Racked by guilt, the King blinds himself and leaves the city in self-imposed exile. Of course, Sophocles was not consciously writing a detective mystery; he was re-telling an ancient myth the theme of which was the punishment of Oedipus' hubris in trying to defy the will of the Gods. Moreover, since every member of the original audiences would already have known the myth, the drama has none of the tension of the modern mystery which derives from the parallel efforts of the detective and the reader to identify the perpetrator. In fact, the main effect of the play is dramatic irony since, unlike the audience, Oedipus does not know the truth which he is about to uncover. Nevertheless, the play has so many of the elements of modern crime fiction that it is remarkable that no other detective mystery would be written for well over two thousand years.

Elizabethan and Jacobean drama is replete with crimes, particularly murder, and the first true novels, written by Daniel Defoe (*The Life of Jonathan Wild* [1725], *Moll Flanders* [1722], etc.), are full of crime and corruption, but are entirely without mystery since the identity of the perpetrator is never in doubt. The *Newgate Calendar*, originally a monthly bulletin of executions, produced by the keeper of Newgate prison in London, was a hugely popular publication between 1750 and 1850 because of its sensational descriptions of the most heinous crimes and the punishments of the (supposedly) guilty. What is missing, at least until the later versions of the Calendar, is any "idea of rational inquiry leading to the containment of crime" (Knight 15). Thus, neither in life nor in fiction is there a single example, official or unofficial, of a detective figure until the middle of the nineteenth century. Malefactors were either caught in the act, or condemned by the unanimous opinion of their neighbors, or they confessed - and no doubt a lot of innocent people were convicted and imprisoned or hanged. Before the

The Detective Story

middle of the nineteenth century, there was also a tendency to romanticize criminals (the mythical ride from London to York of highwayman Dick Turpin is but one example) as rebels against an oppressive government fated, if captured, to endure cruel and unusual punishments.

In fiction, the detective mystery as a genre had its origins in the mid-nineteenth century as an off-shoot of the Romantic Gothic novel, a genre that combined horror and romance: "Prominent features of Gothic fiction include terror (both psychological and physical), mystery, the supernatural, ghosts, haunted houses and Gothic architecture, castles, darkness, death, decay, doubles, madness, secrets and hereditary curses" (Wikipedia). The first Gothic novel is usually taken to be Horace Walpole's *The Castle of Otranto* (1764); Ann Radcliffe's *The Mysteries of Udolpho* (1794) was the most popular example; and Jane Austen satirized the genre in *Northanger Abbey* (1803). King points to Landrum's count of seventy novels published between 1794 and 1854 which had the word "mystery" in their titles, though the term was not, as yet, attached to a single, unsolved crime (19).

Although claims have been made for earlier authors, the American writer Edgar Allan Poe (1809-1849), whose short stories were usually of the horror genre involving death, decay, and madness, is generally credited with writing the first true detective story in 1841. This was the "The Murders in the Rue Morgue" which features a terrible double murder in Paris: a mother and daughter are found brutally murdered in a room where all of the windows are locked from the inside and access to the windows from the outside is clearly impossible given the height of the building and the total absence of handholds. The amateur detective Chevalier C. Auguste Dupin, "the first fictional investigator to rely primarily on deduction from observable facts" (James 33), solves a mystery which completely defeats the French police. Knight explains Poe's contribution to the detective mystery thus:

> [H]is detective stories ... were to bring together for the first time the Gothic melodrama that had been a major element in early crime fiction with the concept of a clever explanatory figure who had not appeared before ... Poe saw the possibilities that others were only half grasping, and ... constructed a form strong enough to predict the possibilities of the genre that was not yet in being. (25-6)

Dupin himself terms his method "ratiocination." His debut was followed by the stories "The Mystery of Marie Rogêt" (1842-3) and "The Purloined Letter" (1845).

In France, the period 1840-1860 saw a rapid expansion of tales involving detective figures by serious authors such as Honoré de Balzac, Alexandre Dumas, and Émile Gaboriau (who is usually credited as "the creator of the detective novel" [Priestman in Hodgson ed. 313]), but in England the genre developed much more slowly. Notable examples include Delf's *The*

Detective's Notebook (1860) and Forrester's *The Female Detective* (1864), but none of these came close to the classic detective mystery. Thus, while Charles Dickens' novels feature both criminals and detectives, both are incidental to the main plots. *Bleak House* (1852-3) includes the character Inspector Bucket, a detective who undertakes several investigations including that of Mr. Tulkinghorn's murder, which he brings to a successful conclusion, and the pursuit of the fleeing Lady Deadlock, who he is not able to find in time to save her life. Dickens' final novel *The Mystery of Edwin Drood* (1870) appears to have a potential detective figure, but it remained unfinished at his death, and so the author's intentions remain unclear.

The credit for a definite movement in English fiction in the direction of the modern detective mystery is usually given to Wilkie Collins. In both *The Woman in White* (1859) and *The Moonstone* (1868) crimes are solved by solid detective work (together with a fair measure of luck and coincidence). *The Moonstone* was termed by T. S. Eliot "the first and greatest of English detective novels," and Dorothy Sayers called it "probably the very finest detective story ever written" (Knight 44). The story involves the disappearance of the fabled diamond called The Moonstone from the room of Rachel Verinder. The local police are baffled and gladly hand over the case to the famous Sergeant Cuff of London who makes great strides toward solving the mystery. However, Cuff is removed from the case at a crucial point and only reappears towards the end of the novel when others have made more progress in explaining the disappearance of the jewel. Both *The Woman in White* and *The Moonstone* employ multiple narrators so there is no single controlling consciousness. The crimes are solved not by one person but by a number of characters whose separate efforts come together in an amazing revelation of the truth and in the just punishment for the offenders.

Even though Collins did not give to the genre the central detective figure which is its single most essential element, P. D. James notes that he "is meticulously accurate in his treatment of medical and forensic details. There is an emphasis on the importance of physical clues - a bloodstained nightdress, a smeared door, a metal chain - and all the clues are made available to the reader ..." (21). What Collins had done, Henry James pointed out, was to bring the sensationalism of the Gothic novel to the familiar landscape of England:

> To Mr. Collins belongs the credit of having introduced into fiction those most mysterious of mysteries, the mysteries which are at our own doors. This innovation ... was fatal to the authority of Mrs. Radcliffe [1764-1823, writer of many Gothic novels most famously *The Mysteries of Udolpho*] and her everlasting castle in the Apennines. What are the Apennines to us or we to the Apennines? Instead of the terrors of "Udolpho," we were treated to the terrors of the

The Detective Story

cheerful country-house and the best London lodgings. And there is no doubt that these were infinitely more terrible. (*The Nation*)

However, neither Inspector Bucket nor Sergeant Cuff, both being middle class members of the official police force, fits the model of the gentleman (or less often the gentlewoman) amateur detective.

In the final decade of the nineteenth century, Sir Arthur Conan Doyle's creation, Sherlock Holmes, achieved great popularity with the British reading public. Doyle wrote that his main achievement was to replace crime novels in which the solution was arrived at by luck or chance through the creation of "a scientific detective who solved cases on his own merits and not through the folly of the criminal" (Hodgson ed. 3). Neilson disagrees, indicating that Doyle's essential contribution to the detective genre was not in the mechanics of the plot or in the nature of criminal detection, but in "his 'humanizing' of the detective. Edgar Allan Poe's C. Auguste Dupin is little more than a disembodied intellect. Collins's Sergeant Cuff is more personable but considerably less skillful. Émile Gaboriau's two early examples, Monsieur Lecoq and Père Tabaret, are ingenious detectives and amiable fellows, but they have almost no distinguishing personal traits" (*Masterplots*). In contrast, Holmes is both a thinker and a man of action, a player of the violin and a talented boxer. Moreover, he is a detective who evidently derives great pleasure from solving puzzles. Not only are both men correct, but Holmes' methods and his personality are seamlessly intertwined.

That Doyle, a voracious reader from his childhood, was well aware of the precursors we have examined is evident in *The Sign of Four* which draws so directly on both Poe and Collins that the charge of plagiarism might be made. Doyle and Crowder suggest that the murder of Bartholomew Sholto in his inaccessible, upper storey room has obvious parallels with, and was indeed inspired by, Poe's "The Murders in the Rue Morgue" (30). They also show the extent of Doyle's debt to Collins by using parallel quotation to prove that he borrowed many of Cuff's physical features in his descriptions of Sherlock Holmes (25). Even more specifically, the novel clearly borrows from *The Moonstone* its central plot device of a fabulous treasure stolen from India and pursued from there by those determined to return it to its 'rightful' owners.

The huge success of the Holmes novels and short stories caused many writers to imitate Doyle's narrative methods. The first half of the twentieth century was the great age of the amateur detective – the individual with supreme insight who could see behind the deceptions of the most cunning criminal. You have to remember that this was a time when the scientific investigation of crime was in its infancy. Solving a crime rested on establishing: Means, Motive and Opportunity (or, to put it another way: How? Why? and When?). In the age before sophisticated forensics, this could be discovered by careful observation, judicious questioning, and the ability to make logical connections. It was also during this period that murder became *the* crime in detective fiction. The number of murders which Holmes investigates is surprisingly small; indeed, some of his most intriguing cases involve no crime at all.

The most famous writer of what came to be called the Golden Age of Detective Fiction, which spanned the time period between World War I and World War II, was Agatha Christie (1891-1976) whose two most popular creations were the Belgian detective Hercule Poirot and the spinster Miss Marple. A contemporary of Christie's, the writer Raymond Chandler (1888-1959), added the American Private Detective to the genre through his hero Philip Marlowe. American detective stories were, from the start, more violent, more 'hard-boiled,' than their English equivalents.

Since the Second World War, much more variety has been introduced into detective fiction, though one trend which is common to most stories of the genre is an increased concern with getting the details of criminal investigation right even as police procedures have become more complex and their methods more scientific. This has resulted in stories that are generally realistic and unromantic. Police Procedurals have a professional policeman or woman as the central figure and follow closely established methods of investigation. A good example are the 87th Precinct novels of Ed McBain featuring New York detective Steve Carella.

Elements of the Classic Detective Mystery:

> What we can expect is a central mysterious crime, usually murder; a closed circle of suspects, each with motive, means and opportunity for the crime; a detective, either amateur or professional, who comes in like an avenging deity to solve it; and, by the end of the book, a solution which the reader should be able to arrive at by logical deduction from clues inserted in the novel with deceptive cunning but essential fairness ... It is an inviolable rule that the detective should never know more than the reader ... (James 9 & 59)

The classic detective mystery contains the following elements:

1. Crime: A crime (normally a murder) is committed by one (or more) of a small number of people, all of whom have possible motives.

2. Setting: The setting is usually an isolated location which effectively restricts the range of possible suspects and makes it equally impossible for the suspects to leave, or for outside help to arrive. (The titles of two of Agatha Christie's novels will illustrate this type of setting: *Murder on the Orient Express* and *Death on the Nile*. In each of these stories, the number of suspects is limited to the people travelling on either the train or the boat respectively. Another of her stories is set in a house on a small island off the

The Detective Story

coast of England.)

3. Characters: There are a fixed and relatively small number of characters each of whom appears to have a motive for the crime as well as the means and opportunity to commit it.

4. Plot structure: The author deliberately plants 'red-herrings' (false clues) in order to confuse the reader, to lead him/her to suspect the wrong people, and to reduce the chances of the reader identifying the one or two significant clues which actually solve the mystery. (Sometimes the writer 'cheats' by allowing the detective access to information which the reader does not have.)

5. The detective: Originally a man, though increasingly a woman, of formidable intellect, the detective is able to piece together the evidence of means, motive and opportunity in order to reveal the guilty party. (Although the genre originated with the talented amateur sleuth [Holmes, Father Brown, Lord Peter Wimsey, Miss Marple, etc.] who outsmarts the official police, as crime detection has become more technical and scientific the sleuth has more often been a professional detective [Inspector Morse, Detective Steve Carella, Detective Chief-Inspector Adam Dalgliesh, etc.]. In such cases, the detective is usually something of an individualist whose approach to solving crimes is very different from that of his colleagues.)

6. The detective's friend: Many detectives, of course, work alone, but a surprising number work together with a close friend. This is normally a man of a practical nature but no skill in detection who performs three functions: he is able to attend to practical matters for which the detective has neither the time nor the inclination; his inability to make logical deductions shows, by contrast, the skills of the detective; and his limited understanding provides the author with an excuse for getting the detective to explain his reasoning. Additionally, the friend (following the tradition inaugurated by Dr. Watson) is often the narrator of the stories.

7. The innocent accused: All of the evidence points to this person, although it is clear to the reader, and to the detective, that he/she is innocent.

8. The Police: Whether the detective figure is an amateur, a private investigator or a policeman, a contrast is drawn between his/her methods and those of the official police. The latter always do things 'by the Book,' which usually leads them to assume the guilt of the most obvious suspect and selectively to use evidence to support their case rather than reviewing all of the evidence to determine who the true culprit is. As a result, they miss everything which is not blindingly obvious. Again, their inability shows up the skills of the detective by contrast.

9. Delayed denouement: Rosemary Jann points to this paradox of detective stories:

> [T]hey move toward [a] solution but exist only so long as closure can be postponed. Our reading pleasure is intimately tied to the suspense that this postponement creates ... Once

Sherlock Holmes Short Stories by Sir Arthur Conan Doyle

> the mystery has been devised, the author's main problem is one of concealment: how to limit the revelation of the solution long enough to maintain the reader's interest. (22-3)

A number of narrative strategies are used to ensure that the solution is kept from the reader. The obtuse narrator (usually a friend of the detective), a person who records every detail without being conscious of what the clues actually are, is the most obvious of these. Others include the false trails followed by the official police, the innocent suspect, and (that most abused of all techniques) the 'red herrings' planted by the author.

10. The climax: The detective gathers together all of the suspects for a final, dramatic explanation of the *who, how* and *why* of the crime which culminates in naming the guilty person, who then confesses.

11. The fate of the guilty person: In more modern stories, he/she is most likely be handed over to the forces of law for trial and punishment, but in earlier stories the amateur detective sometimes allows a higher form of justice to take its course (e.g., the criminal commits suicide or, at the other extreme, is found to have been so justified in what he/she did that he/she is allowed to go free). This is common in the Sherlock Holmes stories.

Of course, writers of detective mysteries have never slavishly used the above points as a template, but one of the great attractions of the genre for readers is its predictability. Most Agatha Christie novels, for example, follow this general formula. Her detectives typically uncover a tangled web of motivation and causation which often goes back several years, sometimes decades. Paradoxically, the Sherlock Holmes stories, whether in the form of novels or short stories, seldom follow the very template that they were inventing (though *The Hound of the Baskervilles* comes closest to it).

Quintessentially, the detective story involves the reader in solving a puzzle. The reader is effectively in a race with the detective to sort out which of the suspects, all of whom appear to have had a motive, actually also had the means and the opportunity to do the murder. Of the characters in the story, the detective alone is able to see through the alibi of the guilty one(s). Therefore, the test of a good detective mystery is that the reader does not guess the identity of the perpetrator despite having been given *all* of the clues in the course of the narrative. When the real criminal is unmasked, the reader should initially be surprised but then realize that it *had* to be him/her all along.

The 'Whodunit?' plot-line, however, by no means exhausts the possibilities of the detective mystery. In some detective stories, it is perfectly clear from the start who the criminal is and what his or her motives are. What remains to be discovered is *how* the crime was committed. Many of the Holmes stories are of this type, the villain being identified immediately by his (hardly ever her) physical description and manner. Perhaps the most famous example is *The Speckled Band*. Helen Stoner's sister has been found dead just before she was to be married, and now the young woman fears for her own life. It is perfectly clear to the reader that the culprit is Helen's violent stepfather, Sir Grimesby Roylott, whose financial motives are not difficult to determine. The mystery lies in watching Holmes discover the manner in which the murder was performed, and specifically what the dying sister meant when she cried, "The band! The speckled band!"

Another variation is a story in which it is immediately clear to the reader who committed the crime and how that person did it, but it is by no means clear what possible motive they had for doing so. Finally (though I am sure that there must be still other variations), there is the plot where the reader is told precisely who did it, and how and why they did it. Since the crime appears to have been meticulously planned and executed (the near-perfect crime), the mystery and accompanying suspense lies in finding out how the detective will discover the truth and bring the criminal to justice. If you have ever seen re-runs of the *Colombo* series, you will know exactly how this variation works.

Any of the variations described above may involve what is often regarded as the holy grail of detective fiction, the 'locked room mystery' in which the crime (again most often murder) has been committed in a room which appears to have been totally secure so that no one could have entered it to commit the crime and (more importantly) no one could possibly have got out of the room having done the deed. Needless to say, crime writers have discovered endless ways of solving this particular mystery. *The Sign of Four* certainly features a murder in a room which appears, at first, to be entirely inaccessible; Doyle's solution borrows heavily from Poe's use of an Ourang-Outang as the perpetrator in "The Murders in the Rue Morgue."

The Sherlock Holmes Canon

Novels:
A Study in Scarlet (1887 in *Beeton's Christmas Annual*),
The Sign of [the] Four (1890 in *Lippincott's Monthly Magazine*),
The Hound of the Baskervilles (1901-02 in *The Strand Magazine*),
The Valley of Fear (1914-15 in *The Strand Magazine*).

Collections of short stories:
The Adventures of Sherlock Holmes (twelve stories from *The Strand Magazine* 1891-2),
The Memoirs of Sherlock Holmes (twelve stories from *The Strand Magazine* 1894),
The Return of Sherlock Holmes (thirteen stories originally published 1903-04),
His Last Bow seven (stories originally published 1908-1917),
The Case-Book of Sherlock Holmes (twelve stories from *The Strand Magazine* 1921-27).

Sherlock Holmes Short Stories by Sir Arthur Conan Doyle

The idea that Doyle began writing fiction because he had so few patients in the practice which he opened in July 1882 at 1, Bush Villas, Elm Grove, Portsmouth, is largely a myth. Even today, any new medical practice takes some time to establish a regular clientele, and at first patients were indeed few and far between. In his first year, Doyle earned only £154, but in his second the figure rose to £250, and in his third to £300, which was around the average income for a doctor in general practice at that time (Booth 95-6). Nor is it true that Doyle was not a particularly good doctor and took little interest in his profession. In fact, he submitted numerous articles to medical journals, proved himself to be, both in terms of his relationships with patients and his medical knowledge, somewhat ahead of his time, and began to specialize in diseases of the eye. However, in 1891, a serious attack of influenza, the failure of his eye specialist practice in Upper Wimpole Street, London, the increasing sums paid for his Holmes stories, and the critical success of his historical novel *The White Company* combined to persuade Doyle that literature would subsequently be his sole means of earning a living. (He would return to medicine during the Boer War as a volunteer.)

In his excellent biography of Doyle, Martin Booth draws on the author's own article in the *Westminster Gazette* (December 1900) to give the following account of the inception of the first Holmes novel, *A Study in Scarlet*:

> [T]he idea of writing about a detective came to him around 1886 when he had read some detective stories and thought they were nonsensical because the plots, often thin, unimaginative and imitative, either revolved around coincidence or relied for their denouement on the authors revealing vital clues that had previously been hidden from the readers ... [T]he detectives themselves were stereotypes who lacked depth and did not display their lines of deduction. He wanted to create, he said, "a scientific detective, who solved cases on his own merits and not through the folly of the criminal. (104)

In the novel's planning stages, the detective was first called Sherringford Holmes then Sherrington Hope, and the doctor Ormond Sacker. Scholars have made many suggestions as to the origin of the names Sherlock Holmes and Dr. John Watson, but as readers we may simply be glad of the change!

Although, Doyle had no thought when writing *A Study in Scarlet* that it would be the first of a series of stories (and certainly not of a series which would span forty years), in all he would write four Holmes novels and fifty-six short stories, all of which appeared as serials or as part of a series in monthly magazines before being published as books. Having been rejected by a number of publishers, the copyright of *A Study in Scarlet* was purchased for £25 by *Beeton's Christmas Annual*. Having sold the copyright, Doyle did not make a penny more on that novel.

The Detective Story

Although the creation of Holmes ultimately made Conan Doyle a very rich man, he saw himself initially as a writer of serious historical fiction (*Micah Clarke* [1889], *The White Company* [1891], *Rodney Stone* [1896] etc.), later on in his career as an historian (*The War in South Africa - Its Causes and Conduct* [1902], *The British Campaign in France and Flanders* [6 vols. 1916-20], etc.), and still later as a writer on Spiritualism (*The New Revelation* [1918], *The Case for Spirit Photography* [1922], etc.). To Doyle, the Holmes stories were merely 'potboilers,' designed to cater to the public taste and, of course, to make money. Once Doyle had secured a steady income from royalties, at various points in his career Doyle would become impatient with the constant public clamor for more Holmes stories. Indeed, as Cox points out, the ending of *The Sign of Four* indicates that Doyle had, at that time, no thought of writing more Sherlock Holmes stories:

> Even though the story demonstrates that Conan Doyle had his formula fully under control, we can see that he had no plans to continue the saga. Watson's marriage will separate Holmes from his chronicler and the 'series' will end with the second and final story. (48)

As with *A Study in Scarlet* which preceded it, *The Sign of Four* was not met with universal approval in contemporary reviews. The Athenaeum review of December 6th, 1890, read:

> A detective story is usually lively reading, but we cannot pretend to think that 'The Sign of Four' is up to the level of the writer's best work. It is a curious medley, full or horrors; and surely those who play at hide and seek with the fatal treasure are a strange company. The wooden-legged convict and his fiendish misshapen little mate, the ghastly twins, the genial prizefighters, the detectives wise and foolish, and the gentle girl whose lover tells the tale, twist in and out together in a merry dance, culminating in that mad and terrible rush down the river which ends the mystery and the treasure. Dr. Doyle's admirers will read the little volume through eagerly enough, but they will hardly care to take it up again.

Although history has proved this judgment to be wide of the mark, the essential criticism that *The Sign of Four* is a mishmash of genres remains valid.

It was the idea of a series of short stories in the monthly magazine *The Strand* which changed literary history, though it remains unclear whether the idea was Doyle's own or that of the magazine's editor. Monthly magazines had been publishing serializations of novels throughout the Victorian era, but the disadvantage of this was that if a reader missed an episode it was very difficult to pick up the plot again. It was the idea of running a series of short stories in *The Strand Magazine* featuring the characters Holmes and Watson which made Holmes such a popular figure. The magazine-reading public liked the self-contained nature of each story combined with the continuity of characters from story to story.

Doyle's earnings for each of his first six stories for *The Strand* was £33 per story, for the next six it rose to £50, and for the next twelve to £83 (Cox 5). Still later, when Doyle's income from his writing gave him the financial security to do so, he made a determined attempt to end the public demand for Holmes stories. In "The Final Problem" (first published in *The Strand Magazine*, December 1893, and as the final story in *The Memoirs of Sherlock Holmes*, 1894) Holmes engages in a life-or-death struggle with his arch enemy and nemesis, the Napoleon of Crime, Professor James Moriarty. Both men apparently fall to their deaths at the Reichenbach Falls in Switzerland. The public was horrified. Doyle and Crowder report that "Over 20,000 people cancelled their subscriptions to *The Strand Magazine* in protest. Young men in London took to wearing black mourning bands. Some young women wore black"  (58). One letter of protest from a female reader opened, "You Brute." To many of his readers, Holmes had become a *real* person.

Eventually, Doyle responded to public demand with the novel *The Hound of the Baskervilles*, a story set before Holmes' death. Generally regarded as the best of the Four Holmes novels, Doyle found that he had merely fueled the demand for more Holmes short stories, and so in "The Adventure of the Empty House" (1903) Holmes returns having spent the three years since his supposed death traveling the world, particularly Tibet and the mystic East. He explains to a relieved Watson that in the struggle he was able to use his knowledge of martial arts to send Moriarty to his death and that he then faked his own plunge over the falls in an effort to convince Moriarty's men, who would certainly seek to revenge the death of their leader, that he had also died.

From the title of the collection *His Last Bow*, it is clear that Doyle was making yet another attempt to wean his public away from Holmes, but one final collection, *The Case-Book of Sherlock Holmes*, was to follow. Of these stories Doyle and Crowder write, "The struggle Doyle had in sustaining the stories is evident; some of these adventures are a bit strained. But others are as good as anything he every wrote" (24). The final Holmes story, "The Adventure of Shoscombe Old Place," first appeared in the *Strand Magazine* of April 1927.

The character of Sherlock Holmes was modeled in great part on Dr. Joseph Bell, Professor of Medicine at Edinburgh University, under whom Doyle studied. Doyle wrote that when Bell met patients:
> He would sit in his receiving room with a face like a Red Indian, and diagnose the people as they came in , before they even opened their mouths. He would tell them details of their past life; and hardly would he ever make a mistake. (Quoted in Doyle and Crowder 32)

Holmes does the same thing both with Watson and with each new client. However, there was also a great deal of the author himself in the character of Holmes including prowess in boxing. In general, however, Doyle gave his diagnostic thinking to Holmes and his love of physical activity to Watson, the man of action and emotion: they are two aspects of their creator.

Introducing Holmes and Watson

The unprecedented popularity of Sherlock Holmes had a great deal to do with Doyle's mastery of the magazine series format, but it goes much deeper than that. Rosemary Jann argues convincingly that:
> Through the character of Holmes, Doyle brilliantly popularized the century's confidence in the uniform operation of scientific laws that allowed the trained observer to deduce causes from effects and what has passed from clues left behind. In the process he offered a powerful image of the scientist as hero, to counter the arrogance of the Victor Frankensteins and Dr. Jekylls of nineteenth-century fiction. (4)

To an age which had lost faith in the consolations of religion, Holmes would satisfy the desire of readers for "a transcendent moral order confirmed by justice and reason and for a society in which power naturally corresponds with virtue" (6). The days when criminals were romanticized rather in the manner of Robin Hood, had long passed. To the literate middle classes, criminals were a threat to their own property and to the stability of a society which allowed them to make a reasonable living. Don Cox suggests Doyle provided the ideal hero to set before a crime-conscious middle class, which would, within six months of the appearance of *A Study in Scarlet* (December 1887), be reeling before the failure of the police to catch Jack the Ripper and

Sherlock Holmes Short Stories by Sir Arthur Conan Doyle

temperamentally ready for a detective who could "foil every criminal" (34).

Sherlock Holmes:

> Much of Holmes's long-term popularity comes from the fact that, as an "outsider," Holmes excites the popular imagination, but, as a defender of the status quo, he is ultimately reassuring. (Neilson)

Throughout the canon, Doyle gives hints about Holmes' early life and family background, but it is unlikely that the author ever worked out a systematic biography for Holmes - rather he gives details as and when necessary with little concern for consistency. Certain conclusions can, however, be drawn. In "The Greek Interpreter," Holmes tells Watson, "'My ancestors were country squires, who appear to have led much the same life as is natural to their class.'" This places Holmes' forebears in the gentry class, rural landowners able to live off the income generated either by leasing out their land for farming and/or by employing a manager to farm it. (Think of the Bennet family in *Pride and Prejudice*.)

On the evidence of his knowledge of Latin and other languages, Holmes clearly had the classical education of a gentleman which means that he would have attended one of the English public schools that existed to educate the male children of the upper middle classes and the aristocracy. There is no mention either of which school or which university he attended (probably either London, Oxford or Cambridge), and it is unclear whether he graduated. To both his school and university, Holmes is indebted for his athletic prowess, particularly in fencing and boxing. Although he was, by his own admission, solitary and unsocial as a student, two former college friends, Victor Trevor and Reginald Musgrave, feature in his later investigations.

Having an inherited income of £400 a year, Holmes had no need to seek paid employment. Thus, in about 1876, after leaving university (with or without a degree), Holmes took rooms in Montague Street having, as he proudly boats to Dr. Watson, "'chosen my own particular profession, or rather created it, for I am the only one in the world ... The only unofficial consulting detective.'" Over the next five years, Holmes spent his time studying criminology in the nearby British Museum Reading Room and developing his consultancy, in the process making a name for himself as an investigator with both the public and with the detectives of the Metropolitan Police whose headquarters was Scotland Yard. The move to 221B Baker Street, sometime early in 1884, is an indication of his greater financial stability, although his need of someone with whom to share expenses shows that he was by no means wealthy. It has no relevance to *The Sign of Four*, but Holmes does have an elder brother, Mycroft, whom he regards as intellectually his superior. Mycroft has some ill-defined position in government administration, though it is implied that he has a power and influence much beyond his actual title.

The Detective Story

Forget any preconceptions you may have of Holmes as a middle-aged man wearing a deerstalker hat. (This image derives from original illustrations by Sidney Paget; Conan Doyle never describes Holmes as wearing one). At the time of *The Sign of Four*, Holmes, like his friend Watson, is in his mid- to late-twenties and very much at the height of his physical powers. Holmes' interest in crime is limited to problem-solving: pitting his wits against those of master criminals provides the stimulation which he needs to live. As Caprettini explains:

> [His] aim is not ethical but logical. To follow traces, to reveal enigmas, to explain mysteries; to bring back the chaos of clues to a world of signs. After this, his mission is over, and the police are the ones to enjoy the moral advantages of success … If he never gives himself up to jealousy, rivalry, narcissism, it is just because he knows that his power does not go beyond the sphere of logos [logical explanation]. (Hodgson ed. 334)

Here a word of warning is in order: almost from his first appearance in print, Holmes has seemed to many readers to be a real person - witness the thousands of letters written over decades to 221B Baker Street (a non-existent address) seeking the great detective's help. Many of those who write about Holmes do so as if Dr. Watson was the *real* author of the tales and Sir Arthur Conan Doyle merely his literary agent. In what has become an intellectual game (the first rule of which is that no one is ever to acknowledge that it *is* a game), Sherlockians have great fun trying to reconcile the inconsistencies and fill in the gaps that they find in the Holmes stories. Such writing is not to be confused with literary criticism.

Dr. John H. Watson:

Holmes and Watson are approximately the same age. John Watson must also have been a product either of the public school system or perhaps of Blackheath Proprietary School (established in 1830 to provide boys whose parents could not afford to send them to a public school with an education of comparable standard), for he reports himself as having played rugby for Blackheath Rugby Club an old-boys' team. He received the degree Doctor of Medicine from London University in 1878 after which he studied at The Royal Victoria Military Hospital at Netley in Hampshire. Upon completion of his course there (probably early in 1880), he left England to join the Fifth Northumberland Fusiliers stationed in India as an Assistant Surgeon.

Having landed in Bombay, however, Watson and some fellow officers found that the regiment had already advanced into Afghanistan. Watson arrived in Candahar (Kandahar or Qandahar) to serve in the Second Anglo-Afghan War (1878 to 1880). After some short time, he was transferred to the Berkshires with which he was serving during the Battle of Maiwand (July

27th, 1880) in which 2,500 British and Indian troops were defeated. British losses were: 21 officers and 948 soldiers killed, and 8 officers and 169 men wounded (britishbattles.com). Watson, who suffered a severe bullet wound, was carried from the field by his orderly, and after a spell at the base hospital in Peshawur, A city in northwest Pakistan, during which his condition improved, he was evacuated to England on the troopship Orontes. The next nine months he spent as an invalid trying to improve his "irretrievably ruined" health.

Since he was unfit for military service, Watson retired on a pension of 11/6d (eleven shillings and six pence) a day. Having recovered somewhat, he came to London where he lived in a private hotel in the Strand, but soon found that his expenditures outran his income. He was introduced to Holmes by a mutual friend who knew that Holmes was looking for someone with whom to share the tenancy of rooms at 221B Baker Street. For both men the arrangement provided "'comfortable rooms at a reasonable price'" (*A Study in Scarlet*). Their first investigation, which Watson would eventually document three years later, began on Tuesday, March 4th, 1884 with the delivery by hand of a letter from Inspector Tobias Gregson of Scotland Yard.

The details of Watson's wounds are confusing and inconsistent since on separate occasions he reports both that he was hit by a rifle bullet in the shoulder and in the leg. The severity of his wound also appears to vary: he returns to England with his health broken, but, though he is seen early in *The Sign of Four* ruefully rubbing his aching leg, only a few hours later he confidently pronounces himself up to a six-mile walk. In *The Hound of the Baskervilles*, set a few years later, his ability to walk long distances in rugged Dartmoor suggests a full recovery!

Holmes is the stereotypical bachelor, but Watson has an eye for the ladies. In *The Sign of Four*, he speaks of himself as having had experience of women in "'many nations and three separate continents,'" which has led to inconclusive speculation about his travels prior to meeting Holmes and quite what the nature of his knowledge of women was. In *The Sign of Four* we hear of his proposed marriage to Mary Morstan which will cause him to vacate the Baker Street rooms. There is every indication that his marriage was happy, although it lasted only about ten years. Watson would remain a widower until around 1912 when he must have re-married for Holmes reports, "the good Watson has deserted me for a wife, the only selfish action which I can recall in our association" ("The Blanched Soldier"). Clearly either Holmes' memory or Doyle's is here in error since this was Watson's *second* marriage and hence his second desertion of his friend. Following his marriage to Mary Morstan, Watson would set up a medical practice in Paddington which proved moderately successful, although in the stories he always seems both willing and able to hand his practice over to a locum whenever Holmes needs his help on a case.

The Detective Story

Since both Holmes and Watson are gentlemen by birth and education, they represent the very essence of traditional British values of honor and fair-play. As Hodgson explains, "Both Holmes and Watson share with their creator an unwavering devotion to the chivalric code, a sure sense of the values and duties of a gentleman" (6). Unlike the official police, they are often able to apply a code which transcends the dictates of the law.

Sherlock Holmes Short Stories by Sir Arthur Conan Doyle

The Red-Headed League

Structure of the Story:

The story falls into the following sections:

- Setting the scene in Holmes' Baker Street rooms;
- Watson cannot deduce anything about the client, but Holmes can:
- The statement of the mystery by the client;
- Holmes questions the client;
- Holmes thinks through the problem;
- The investigation;
- Watson can't deduce anything from the crime-scene, but Holmes can;
- Setting the trap and catching the criminal(s);
- Holmes explains how he solved the mystery.

Activity: Locate in the text where each section begins and ends.

The Detective's Methods:

The main clues are:

1. Mr. Wilson says that his only assistant, Vincent Spaulding, was willing to accept the job "'for half wages so as to learn the business ... I know very well that he could ... earn twice what I am able to give him.'"

2. Mr. Wilson mentions one fault which his assistant has: "'Snapping away with a camera ... then diving down into the cellar ... to develop his pictures.'" To Holmes, the fact that the assistant spends a lot of time in the cellar is significant.

3. Mr. Wilson says that before Spaulding came, he very seldom went out of the shop: "'I am a very stay-at-home man ... I was often weeks on end without putting my foot over the doormat.'" This gives Holmes the explanation of the purpose of the Red-headed League.

4. Mr. Wilson reports that it was Spaulding who first brought the Red-headed League to his attention, that he seemed to know quite a lot about it and that he encouraged Mr. Wilson to apply: "'Spaulding came down into the office just this day eight weeks with this very paper in his hand ... [He told me that] the League was founded by an American millionaire, Ezekiah Hopkins ... [and assured me] "Now if you cared to apply, Mr. Wilson, you would just walk in." ... When I saw how many were waiting, I would have given up in despair, but Spaulding would not hear of it ... he pushed and pulled and butted until he got me through the crowd, and right up to the steps which led to the office.'" This tells Holmes a great deal about the assistant's motivation.

5. Mr. Wilson noted a different attitude from the person doing the interviewing when he appeared before him: "'when our turn came, the little man was more favourable to me than to any of the others.'" It's obviously a fix!

6. The terms of Mr. Wilson's membership of the Red-headed League are that he has ""'to be in the office, or at least the building, the whole time [i.e. 10 am - 2 pm].'"" When Mr. Wilson objects that he has ""'a business already,'"" Spaulding is very anxious to reassure him: ""'Oh, never mind about that Mr. Wilson ... I shall be able to look after that for you.'"" Once he has joined the League, steps are taken to check that he is keeping to the terms: "'Mr. Duncan Ross ... would drop in from time to time ... By degrees ... [he] took to coming in only once of a morning, and then, after a time, he didn't come at all.'"

7. Holmes is struck by one detail of Mr. Wilson's description of Spaulding: "'[He] has a white splash of acid on his forehead.' He sat up in his chair in considerable excitement. 'I thought as much...'" This is one of those examples

of the author cheating because the detective knows something that the reader cannot possibly know. (We only find out after the case has been solved.)

8. Holmes and Watson go to see the neighborhood of Mr. Wilson's shop and Watson reports that "[Holmes] thumped vigorously upon the pavement with his stick two or three times." Holmes is trying to discover whether the ground under the pavement is solid or hollow. Why?

9. Having engaged the assistant Vincent Spaulding in conversation, Holmes draws Watson's attention to the knees of his trousers. When Watson asks "'And what did you see?'" Holmes replies, "'What I expected to see.'" Holmes is often able to find evidence because he has already formed a theory about the crime. What did he expect to see and why?

10. In studying the buildings close to Mr. Wilson's shop, Holmes notes "'the Coburg branch of the City and Suburban Bank.'" It is not too hard to see that this is the motive for and the target of the planned crime.

The Red-Headed League

Holmes and the Regular Police:

In this story the official policeman is Mr. Peter Jones of Scotland Yard. He appears towards the end of the story having been contacted by Holmes.

Activity: Answer these questions:
1. What is Jones' attitude to Holmes and to his methods of solving crimes? (Look carefully at the importance of the following words and phrases: "'... his own little methods ... just a little too theoretical and fantastic ... he has the makings of a detective ...'")

2. What is Holmes' attitude to Jones?

3. Why does Holmes involve the regular police in this case?

Sherlock Holmes Short Stories by Sir Arthur Conan Doyle

Activity: For each of the clues write (on the activity sheet) about what Holmes was able to deduce and how it helped him to solve the mystery. To give you an idea, here are some done for you:

Clue #1

Mr. Wilson says that his only assistant, Vincent Spaulding, was willing to accept the job "'for half wages so as to learn the business ... I know very well that he could ... earn twice what I am able to give him.'"

Deduction: This suggests to Holmes that the assistant, Vincent Spaulding, had a secret reason for wanting to work for Mr. Wilson. Holmes is sure at once that he did not accept low wages simply to learn the business as he claimed.

Clue #7

Holmes is struck by one detail of Mr. Wilson's description of Spaulding: "'[He] has a white splash of acid on his forehead.' He sat up in his chair in considerable excitement. 'I thought as much...'" This is one of those examples of the author cheating because the detective knows something that the reader cannot possibly know.

Deduction: It is clear that Holmes recognizes Mr. Wilson's description of Vincent Spaulding as that of a dangerous criminal. This makes Holmes certain that the Red-headed League was set up so that the man calling himself Spaulding could commit a serious crime.

The Red-Headed League

Be a detective... "The Red headed League"

Activity: For each of the clues, write a clear account of what Holmes was able to deduce and how it helped him to solve the mystery.

Clue #1	Mr. Wilson says that his only assistant, Vincent Spaulding, was willing to accept the job "'for half wages so as to learn the business ... I know very well that he could ... earn twice what I am able to give him.'"
Deduction	
Clue #2	Mr. Wilson mentions one fault which his assistant has: "'Snapping away with a camera ... then diving down into the cellar ... to develop his pictures.'" To Holmes, the fact that the assistant spends a lot of time in the cellar is significant.
Deduction	
Clue #3	Mr. Wilson says that before Spaulding came, he very seldom went out of the shop: "'I am a very stay-at-home man ... I was often weeks on end without putting my foot over the doormat.'" This gives Holmes the explanation to the purpose of the Red-headed League.
Deduction	

Clue #4	Mr. Wilson reports that it was Wilson who first brought the Red-headed League to his attention, that he seemed to know quite a lot about it and that he encouraged Mr. Wilson to apply: "'Spaulding came down into the office just this day eight weeks with this very paper in his hand ... [He told me that] the League was founded by an American millionaire, Ezekiah Hopkins ... [and assured me] "Now if you cared to apply, Mr. Wilson, you would just walk in." ... When I saw how many were waiting, I would have given up in despair, but Spaulding would not hear of it ... he pushed and pulled and butted until he got me through the crowd, and right up to the steps which led to the office.'" This tells Holmes a great deal about the assistant's motivation.
Deduction	
Clue #5	Mr. Wilson noted a different attitude from the person doing the interviewing when he appeared before him: "'when our turn came, the little man was more favourable to me than to any of the others.'"
Deduction	

The Red-Headed League

Clue #6	The terms of Mr. Wilson's membership of the Red-headed League are that he has "'"to be in the office, or at least the building, the whole time [i.e. 10 am - 2 pm].'" When Mr. Wilson objects that he has "'"a business already,"'" Spaulding is very anxious to reassure him: "'"Oh, never mind about that Mr. Wilson ... I shall be able to look after that for you."'" Once he has joined the League, steps are taken to check that he is keeping to the terms: "'Mr. Duncan Ross ... would drop in from time to time ... By degrees ... [he] took to coming in only once of a morning, and then, after a time, he didn't come at all.'"
Deduction	
Clue # 7	Holmes is struck by one detail of Mr. Wilson's description of Spaulding: "'[He] has a white splash of acid on his forehead.' He sat up in his chair in considerable excitement. 'I thought as much...'" This is one of those examples of the author cheating because the detective knows something that the reader cannot possibly know.
Deduction	

24

Sherlock Holmes Short Stories by Sir Arthur Conan Doyle

Clue # 8	Holmes and Watson go to see the neighborhood of Mr. Wilson's shop and Watson reports that "[Holmes] thumped vigorously upon the pavement with his stick two or three times." Holmes is trying to discover whether the ground under the pavement is solid or hollow. Why?
Deduction	
Clue # 9	Having engaged the assistant Vincent Spaulding in conversation, Holmes draws Watson's attention to the knees of his trousers. When Watson asks "'And what did you see?'" Holmes replies, "'What I expected to see.'" Holmes is often able to find evidence because he has already formed a theory about the crime.
Deduction	
Clue # 10	In studying the buildings close to Mr. Wilson's shop, Holmes notes "'the Coburg branch of the City and Suburban Bank.'" It is not too hard to see that this is the motive for and the target of the planned crime
Deduction	

The Red-Headed League

Plot Graph for the Sherlock Holmes Short Story:

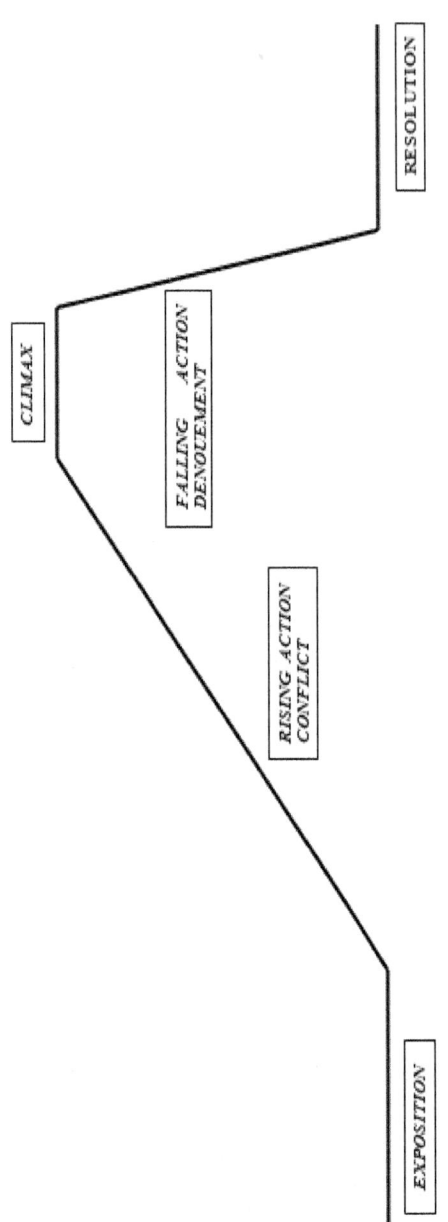

26

Sherlock Holmes Short Stories by Sir Arthur Conan Doyle

The Man with The Twisted Lip

Structure of the Story:

The story falls into the following sections:

- Watson explains how he got involved in the case;
- A description of the criminal underworld of London;
- The statement of the mystery (in this case given by Holmes to Watson);
- Holmes questions the client;
- Holmes thinks about the problem;
- Watson's poor powers of deduction are contrasted to Holmes' skills;
- The solution (in this case leading to the discovery of the missing man);
- Holmes explains how he solved the crime.

Activity: Locate in the text where each section begins and ends.

The Detective's Methods:

The main clues are:

The client's narrative (as repeated by Holmes):

1. "'One singular point which struck her quick feminine eye was that, although he wore some dark coat, such as he had started up to town in, he had on neither collar nor necktie.'" Although it is too soon for either the reader or Holmes to recognize it, the solution to the whole mystery lies in this little observation.

2. "'[T]races of blood were to be seen on the window sill, and several scattered drops were visible upon the wooden floor of the bedroom.'" This evidence may suggest violence to the police, but what Holmes notes is that there was very little blood.

3. "'Thrust away behind a curtain in the front room were all the clothes of Mr. Neville St. Clair, with the exception of his coat ... There were no signs of violence upon any of the garments.'"

4. "'[A]s he is a piteous spectacle a small rain of charity descends into the greasy leather cap ... I have been surprised at the harvest which he has reaped in a short time.'" Again, this little observation by Holmes is the key to unlocking the mystery of St. Clair's disappearance, but at this point in the story Holmes doesn't understand it.

5. "'[S]ome bloodstains upon his right shirt-sleeve, but he pointed to his ring finger, which had been cut near the nail.'"

6. Mrs. St. Clair receives a letter in her husband's handwriting and enclosed with it: "'There was a ring. His signet ring.'" Mrs. St. Clair identifies the writing on the letter as her husband's: "'his hand when he wrote hurriedly ... I know it well.'"

7. Mrs. St. Clair tells Holmes that: "'On the very day that I saw him last he cut himself in the bathroom.'" This makes it absolutely clear to Holmes where St. Clair is. How?

Sherlock Holmes Short Stories by Sir Arthur Conan Doyle

Holmes and the Regular Police:

In this story the official policeman is Inspector Bradstreet of Bow Street. He appears quite late in the story when Holmes goes to unmask St. Clair's disguise at the cells. (Find the paragraph beginning: "In town the early risers...")

Activity: Answer this question:
From the way Holmes is treated by the official policemen whom he meets, what do you learn about the way they feel about him?

Activity: For each of the clues, write a clear account (on the activity sheet) about what Holmes was able to deduce and how it helped him to solve the mystery. To give you an idea of what you have to do, here are some done for you:

Clue #1
"'On singular point which struck her quick feminine eye was that, although he wore some dark coat, such as he had started up to town in, he had on neither collar nor necktie.'" Although it is too soon for either the reader or Holmes to recognize it, the solution to the whole mystery lies in this little observation.

Deduction: Although this does not make sense to Holmes at first, Mrs. St. Clair actually caught her husband in the act of changing back from his beggar's disguise into his normal clothes. He had clearly taken off his make-up but had not yet changed into his city clothes.

Clue #4
"'[A]s he is a piteous spectacle a small rain of charity descends into the greasy leather cap ... I have been surprised at the harvest which he has reaped in a short time.'" Again, this little observation by Holmes is the key to unlocking the mystery of St. Clair's disappearance, but at this point in the story Holmes doesn't understand it.

Deduction: This observation of by Holmes' provides the key to the whole mystery. It is clear that the beggar made a lot of money every day - enough to convince his wife that he had a good job in the city. The beggar and St. Clair are one person.

The Man with the Twisted Lip

Be a detective..."The Man with the Twisted Lip"

Activity: For each of the clues, write a clear account of what Holmes was able to deduce and how it helped him to solve the mystery.

Clue #1	"'On singular point which struck her quick feminine eye was that, although he wore some dark coat, such as he had started up to town in, he had on neither collar nor necktie.'" Although it is too soon for either the reader or Holmes to recognize it, the solution to the whole mystery lies in this little observation.
Deduction	
Clue #2	"'[T]races of blood were to be seen on the window sill, and several scattered drops were visible upon the wooden floor of the bedroom.'" This evidence may suggest violence to the police, but what Holmes notes is that there was very little blood.
Deduction	

Clue #3	"'Thrust away behind a curtain in the front room were all the clothes of Mr. Neville St. Clair, with the exception of his coat ... There were no signs of violence upon any of the garments.'"
Deduction	
Clue #4	"'[A]s he is a piteous spectacle a small rain of charity descends into the greasy leather Cap ... I have been surprised at the harvest which he has reaped in a short time.'" Again, this little observation by Holmes is the key to unlocking the mystery of St. Clair's disappearance, but at this point in the story Holmes doesn't understand it.
Deduction	

Clue #5	"'[S]ome bloodstains upon his right shirt-sleeve, but he pointed to his ring finger, which had been cut near the nail.'"
Deduction	
Clue #6	Mrs. St. Clair receives a letter in her husband's handwriting and enclosed with it: "'There was a ring. His signet ring.'" Mrs. St. Clair identifies the writing on the letter as her husband's: "'his hand when he wrote hurriedly ... I know it well.'"
Deduction	
Clue # 7	Mrs. St. Clair tells Holmes that: "'On the very day that I saw him last he cut himself in the bathroom.'" This makes it absolutely clear to Holmes where St. Clair is. How?
Deduction	

Sherlock Holmes Short Stories by Sir Arthur Conan Doyle

Plot Graph for the Sherlock Holmes Short Story:

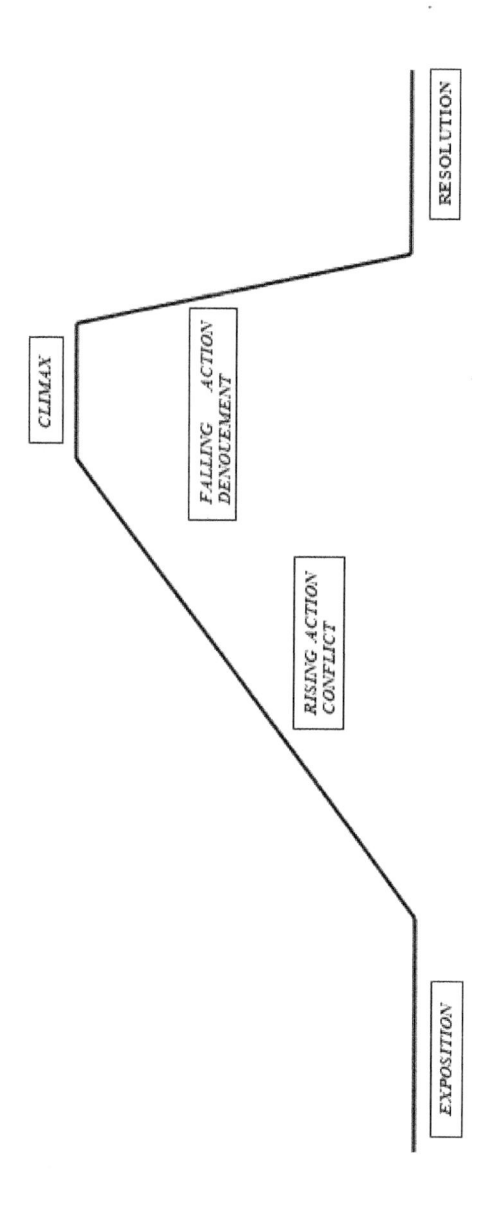

EXPOSITION

RISING ACTION
CONFLICT

CLIMAX

FALLING ACTION
DENOUEMENT

RESOLUTION

Sherlock Holmes Short Stories by Sir Arthur Conan Doyle

The Speckled Band

The Structure of the Story:

The story falls into the following sections:

- Watson explains how he got involved in the case and why he records it now;
- Setting the scene in Holmes' Baker Street rooms;
- Holmes displays his powers of deduction;
- The statement of the mystery (in this case by the client);
- Holmes questions the client;
- Holmes discusses the problem with Watson and forms a theory;
- The villain comes to Holmes' rooms and threatens him;
- Holmes does some investigation in London;
- Holmes travels with Watson to the crime-scene to investigate;
- The solution (in this case leading to the murderer falling victim to his own plan);
- Holmes explains how he solved the case.

Activity: Locate in the text where each section begins and ends.

The Speckled Band

The Detective's Methods:

The clues are:

1. Helen Stoner tells Holmes that when her mother married Dr. Roylott: "'She had a considerable sum of money, not less than a thousand a year, and this she bequeathed to Dr. Roylott entirely whilst we resided with him, with a provision that a certain annual sum should be allowed to each of us in the event of our marriage.'" Holmes later discovers more about this legacy: "'The total income ... is ... not more than £750. Each daughter can claim an income of £250, in the case of marriage ... even one of them [marrying] would cripple him...'"

2. Helen says of her sister Julia's engagement: "'My stepfather learned of the engagement when my sister returned [from Miss Honoria Wesphail's], and offered no objection to the marriage; but within a fortnight of the day which had been fixed for the wedding, the terrible event occurred...'"

3. Helen's describes the location of the three bedrooms: "'The bedrooms ... are on the ground floor ... the first is Dr. Roylott's, the second my sister's, and the third my own. There is no communication between them, but they all open into the same corridor.'"

4. The greatest single clue to the mystery is: "'That fatal night ... my sister was troubled by the smell of the strong Indian cigars [which Dr. Roylott smoked].'"

5. Helen heard a whistle: "'As I opened my door, I seemed to hear a low whistle, such as my sister described...'" Immediately afterwards, Helen heard: "'a clanging sound, as if a mass of metal had fallen.'"

6. Julia's dying words and actions were: "''O, my God! Helen! It was the band! The speckled band!' ... and she stabbed with her finger into the air in the direction of the Doctor's room...'"

7. Helen has been moved into Julia's old room because of building work on her own room. Holmes observes that there seemed to be no need for any building work to be done and Helen agrees: "'I believe that it was an excuse to move me from my room.'"

8. Holmes discovers that the "'thick bell rope'" which hangs down onto the pillow of the bed is a dummy: "'You see now that it is fastened to a hook just above where the little opening of the ventilator is.'" He also discovers that the ventilator connects to Dr. Roylott's room. Both alterations were made just before the death of Julia.

Sherlock Holmes Short Stories by Sir Arthur Conan Doyle

9. In Dr. Roylott's room Holmes finds: "a small saucer of milk" on the top of "a large iron safe" and "a small dog lash ... The lash, however, was curled upon itself, and tied so as to make a loop of whipcord."

10. Holmes observes that the bed was "'clamped to the floor ... The lady could not move her bed. It must always be in the same relative position to the ventilator and the rope...'"

Holmes and the Regular Police:

When Dr. Roylott accuses Holmes of being part of the official police force," 'Holmes the Scotland Yard jack-in-office,'" Holmes says to Watson, "'Fancy his having the insolence to confound me with the official detective force!'"

Activity: Answer this question:

What does Holmes' reaction tell us of his attitude towards the official police?

Activity:
For each of the clues write a clear account (on the activity sheet) of what Holmes was able to deduce and how it helped him to solve the mystery. To give you an idea of what you have to do, here are some done for you:

Clue #1
Helen Stoner tells Holmes that when her mother married Dr. Roylott: "'She had a considerable sum of money, not less than a thousand a year, and this she bequeathed to
Dr. Roylott entirely whilst we resided with him, with a provision that a certain annual sum should be allowed to each of us in the event of our marriage.'" Holmes later discovers more about this legacy: "'The total income ... is ... not more than £750. Each daughter can claim an income of £250, in the case of marriage ... even one of them [marrying] would cripple him...'"

Deduction: In this story there is never any doubt about who the criminal is: Dr. Roylott killed Julia and he is trying to kill Helen. His motive for wanting them dead is to keep all of the money which his wife left to all three in her will.

Clue# 6.

Julia's dying words and actions were: "'"O, my God! Helen! It was the band! The speckled band!' ... and she stabbed with her finger into the air in the direction of the Doctor's room...'"

Deduction: At first Holmes misunderstands this clue. He thinks that it is a reference to the speckled handkerchiefs which the gypsies wear. He later understands that it was a very accurate description of the snake which killed Helen.

Sherlock Holmes Short Stories by Sir Arthur Conan Doyle

Be a detective... "The Speckled Band"

Activity: For each of the clues, write a clear account of what Holmes was able to deduce and how it helped him to solve the mystery.

Clue #1	Helen Stoner tells Holmes that when her mother married Dr. Roylott: "'She had a considerable sum of money, not less than a thousand a year, and this she bequeathed to Dr. Roylott entirely whilst we resided with him, with a provision that a certain annual sum should be allowed to each of us in the event of our marriage.'" Holmes later discovers more about this legacy: "'The total income ... is ... not more than £750. Each daughter can claim an income of £250, in the case of marriage ... even one of them [marrying] would cripple him...'"
Deduction	
Clue #2	Helen says of her sister's engagement: "'My stepfather learned of the engagement when my sister returned [from Miss Honoria Wesphail's], and offered no objection to the marriage; but within a fortnight of the day which had been fixed for the wedding, the terrible event occurred...'"
Deduction	

The Speckled Band

Clue #3	Helen describes the location of the three bedrooms: "'The bedrooms ... are on the ground floor ... the first is Dr. Roylott's, the second my sister's, and the third my own. There is no communication between them, but they all open into the same corridor.'"
Deduction	
Clue #4	The greatest single clue to the mystery is: "'That fatal night ... my sister was by the smell of the strong Indian cigars [which Dr. Roylott smoked].'"
Deduction	

Sherlock Holmes Short Stories by Sir Arthur Conan Doyle

Clue #5	Helen heard a whistle: "'As I opened my door, I seemed to hear a low whistle, such as my sister described...'" Immediately afterwards, Helen heard: "'a clanging sound, as if a mass of metal had fallen.'"
Deduction	
Clue #6	Julia's dying words and actions were: "'"O, my God! Helen! It was the band! The speckled band!' ... and she stabbed with her finger into the air in the direction of the Doctor's room...'"
Deduction	
Clue # 7	Helen has been moved into Julia's old room because of building work on her own room. Holmes observes that there seemed to be no need for any building work to be done and Helen agrees: "'I believe that it was an excuse to move me from my room.'"
Deduction	

The Speckled Band

Clue # 8	Holmes discovers that the "'thick bell rope'" which hangs down onto the pillow of the bed is a dummy: "'You see now that it is fastened to a hook just above where the little opening of the ventilator is.'" He also discovers that the ventilator connects to Dr. Roylott's room. Both alterations were made just before the death of Julia.
Deduction	
Clue # 9	In Dr. Roylott's room Holmes finds: "a small saucer of milk" on the top of "a large iron safe" and "a small dog lash ... The lash, however, was curled upon itself, and tied so as to make a loop of whipcord."
Deduction	
Clue # 10	Holmes observes that the bed was "'clamped to the floor ... The lady could not move her bed. It must always be in the same relative position to the ventilator and the rope...'"
Deduction	

Sherlock Holmes' Copy of the Will of Mrs. Roylott

Activity: Here is a (hypothetical) copy of the will which Dr. Roylott's wife made. It also has Holmes own notes on it. Read the story carefully and fill in the gaps.

The Last Will and Testament of Mrs. Roylott (formerly Mrs. _____, widow of _____).

Being of sound mind and body, I leave the following to Dr. Roylott.:

I have a number of investments. At present I earn from them almost £1,100 each year. I leave all of this yearly income to Dr. Roylott.

I ask only that he takes care of my dear daughters _____ and _____, until the time comes for them to _____.

When each daughter _____, she is to be given £_____ a year. This money is to be taken from the income of my investments and what remains is to go to Dr. Roylott.

When both daughters are married, my dear husband should still have an income of £_____ each year.

Signed,
Mrs. Roylott

The Speckled Band

When Mrs. Roylott made her will her investments were worth nearly £1,100 a year. She invested mainly in farming. Since then _____ have fallen. The income from the investments is now only £_____.

This means that: if one daughter married Dr. Roylott would be left with only £_____, and if both daughters were to marry, he would have only £_____.

Here we have the man's motive: he could not afford to lose even what one daughter's marriage would cost him.

Sherlock Holmes Short Stories by Sir Arthur Conan Doyle

Plot Graph for the Sherlock Holmes Short Story:

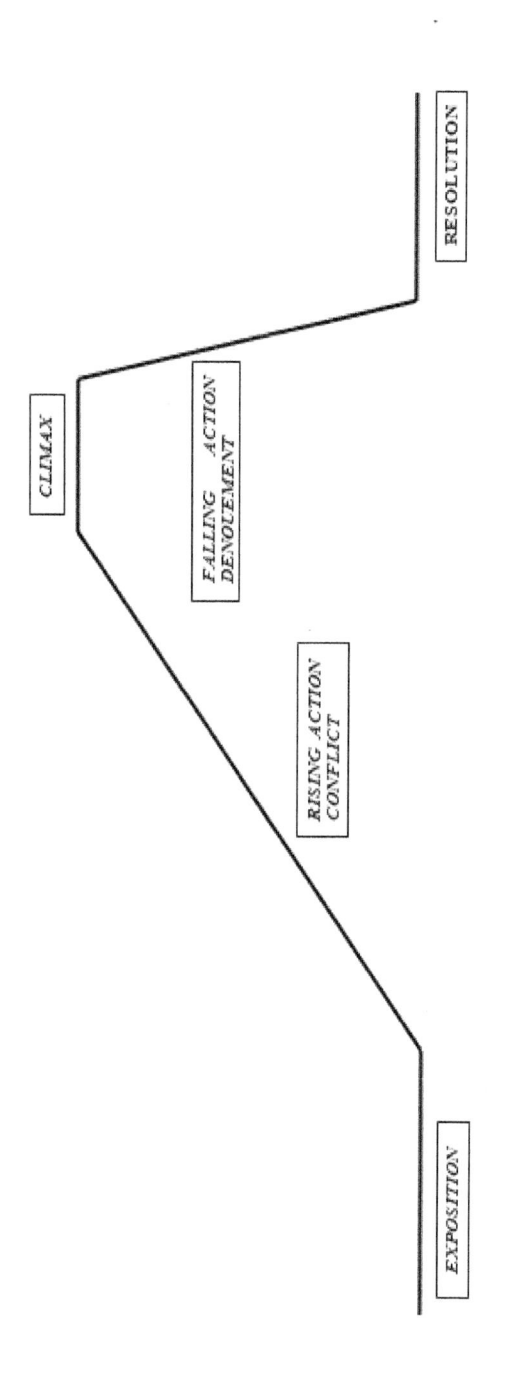

- EXPOSITION
- RISING ACTION / CONFLICT
- CLIMAX
- FALLING ACTION / DENOUEMENT
- RESOLUTION

Sherlock Holmes Short Stories by Sir Arthur Conan Doyle

Silver Blaze

The Structure of the Story:

The story falls into the following sections:

- Watson's explanation of how he came to be involved in the case;
- Holmes and Watson travel to the scene;
- Watson's inferior powers of deduction are contrasted to those of Holmes;
- The statement of the mystery (in this case given by Holmes to Watson);
- Holmes investigates the crime scene and questions the witnesses;
- The solution (in this case leading to the quite unexpected return of Silver Blaze);
- Holmes' explanation of the clues.

Activity: Locate in the text where each section begins and ends.

Silver Blaze

The Detective's Methods:

The clues are:

The client's narrative (in this case given by Holmes to Watson);

1. Fitzroy Simpson is the obvious suspect, and there is much to suggest that he drugged the stable-boy with powdered opium: "'The girl ... saw that the stranger was leaning through the window ... The boy locked the door before he left it. The window ... was not large enough for a man to get through.'" However, Holmes notes one important clue. The supper which Edith Baxter carries down to the stable-boy: "'consisted of a dish of curried mutton.'"

2. "'Mrs. Straker, waking at one in the morning, found that he [Mr. Straker] was dressing ... he said that he ... intended to walk down to the stables to see that all was well.'"

3. "'His head had been shattered by a savage blow from some heavy weapon, and he was wounded in the thigh where there was a long, clean cut, inflicted evidently by some very sharp instrument ... in his right hand he held a small knife, which was clotted with blood ... in his left he grasped a red and black silver cravat ... worn on the preceding evening by the stranger.'"

Holmes' questioning:

4. "'When confronted with the cravat he turned very pale, and was utterly unable to account for its presence in the hand of the murdered man.'"

5. Watson's medical knowledge is able to identify the knife which injured Straker as "'a cataract knife,'" which Holmes describes as: "'A very delicate blade devised for very delicate work.'"

6. The key clue is a piece of paper which was in Straker's pocket: "'A milliner's account for £37/15/- made out by Madame Lesurier of Bond Street to William Darbyshire. Mrs. Straker tells us that Darbyshire was a friend of her husband's...'"

The investigation:

7. As so often, Holmes is able to find something at the scene of the crime because he knows what to look for: "It was a wax vesta [a match], half buried... 'I cannot think how I came to overlook it,' said the Inspector ... 'I only saw it because I was looking for it.' [said Holmes]."

8. Locating the whereabouts of Silver Blaze is a simple matter of reading the tracks left in the soft ground: "A man's track was visible beside the horse's ... It ended at the paving asphalt which led to the gates of the Capleton stables." Holmes' questioning:

Sherlock Holmes Short Stories by Sir Arthur Conan Doyle

9. "'three of the sheep have gone lame, sir.'"

10. "'Is there any point to which you would wish to draw my attention?' 'To the curious incident of the dog in the night-time.' 'The dog did nothing in the night-time.' 'That was the curious incident,' remarked Sherlock Holmes." (This dialogue has become a classic in detective fiction.)

Silver Blaze

Holmes and the Regular Police:

In this story the official police are represented by Inspector Gregory. As usual, the methods of the official police lead them to suspect the wrong man.

Activity: Answer these questions:

1. What is Holmes' opinion of the abilities of Inspector Gregory?

2. What opinion does Inspector Gregory appear to have of Holmes?

3. Holmes frequently puts himself above the law in deciding who should and who should not be punished. Explain how he does so in this story.

Activity:
For each of the clues write a clear account (on the activity sheet) about what Holmes was able to deduce and how it helped him to solve the mystery. Here is one done for you:

Clue #6.
The key clue is a piece of paper which was in Straker's pocket: "'A milliner's account for £37/15/- made out by Madame Lesurier of Bond Street to William Darbyshire. Mrs. Straker tells us that Darbyshire was a friend of her husband's...'"

Deduction: This story is a classic *who-done-it* in which the man with motive, means and opportunity is the most unlikely suspect. It is this piece of evidence, however, which indicates to Holmes that Straker has a motive. It is clear to Holmes that "Mr. Darbyshire" is an invention, another name used by Straker. He establishes that the women's clothes were not bought for Straker's wife, which leads to the deduction that Straker had a mistress – someone with very expensive tastes which Straker found very difficult to pay for. He could make a lot of money by betting against Silver Blaze having made the horse slightly lame.

Sherlock Holmes Short Stories by Sir Arthur Conan Doyle

Be a detective... "Silver Blaze"

Activity: For each of the clues, write a clear account of what Holmes was able to deduce and how it helped him to solve the mystery.

Clue #1	Fitzroy Simpson is the obvious suspect, and there is much to suggest that he drugged the stable-boy with powdered opium: "'The girl ... saw that the stranger was leaning through the window ... The boy locked the door before he left it. The window ... was not large enough for a man to get through.'" However, Holmes notes one important clue. The supper which Edith Baxter carries down to the stable-boy: "'consisted of a dish of curried mutton.'"
Deduction	
Clue #2	"'Mrs. Straker, waking at one in the morning, found that he [Mr. Straker] was dressing ... he said that he ... intended to walk down to the stables to see that all was well.'"
Deduction	

51

Clue #3	"'His head had been shattered by a savage blow from some heavy weapon, and he was wounded in the thigh where there was a long, clean cut, inflicted evidently by some very sharp instrument ... in his right hand he held a small knife, which was clotted with blood ... in his left he grasped a red and black silver cravat ... worn on the preceding evening by the stranger.'"
Deduction	

Sherlock Holmes Short Stories by Sir Arthur Conan Doyle

Plot Graph for the Sherlock Holmes Short Story:

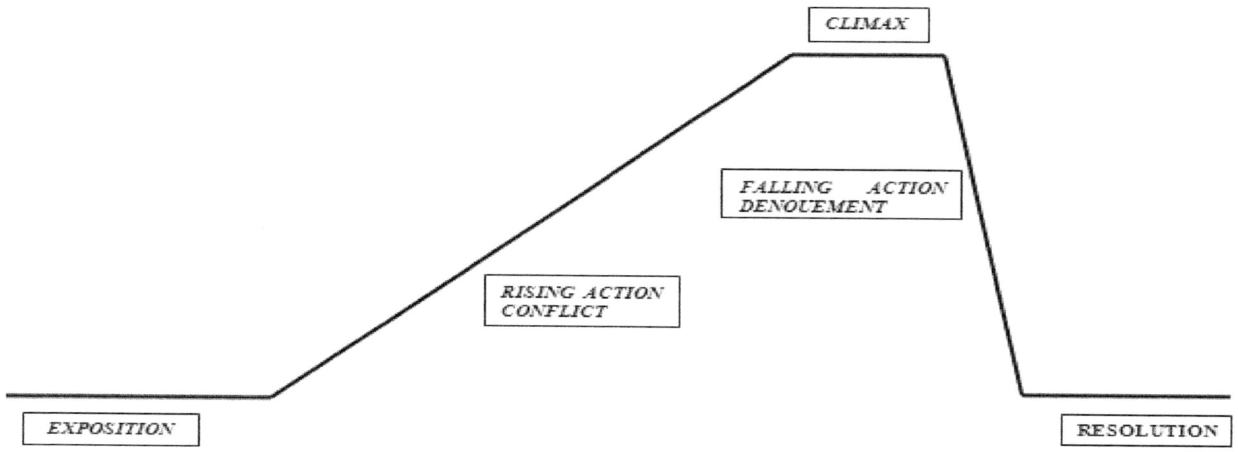

- EXPOSITION
- RISING ACTION / CONFLICT
- CLIMAX
- FALLING ACTION / DENOUEMENT
- RESOLUTION

Sherlock Holmes Short Stories by Sir Arthur Conan Doyle

The Cardboard Box

The Structure of the Story:

The story falls into the following sections:
- Watson's justification of the sensational nature of the story;
- Setting the scene in Holmes' Baker Street rooms;
- Holmes' powers of deduction are illustrated;
- The statement of the mystery (in this case read by Holmes from the
- newspaper and from Inspector Lestrade's letter);
- Holmes and Watson travel to the scene;
- The investigation;
- Holmes questions the witness, Miss Cushing;
- Holmes' explanation of the clues;
- The murderer's statement.

Activity: Locate in the text where each section begins and ends.

The Adventure of the Cardboard Box

The Detective's Methods:

The clues are:

The investigation:

1. The official police suspect a prank by some medical students. Holmes is quickly able to dismiss this possibility from his mind. He is able to deduce some things about the person who cut off the ears from details about the package in which the ears were sent. Although he draws these details to the attention of Inspector Lestrade, the Inspector fails to see their significance. Here are the points: "'It is a piece of tarred twine ... this knot is of a very peculiar character ... Brown paper, with a distinct smell of coffee.'"

2. Two other factors help him to disprove the medical student theory: "'They have been cut off with a blunt instrument ... carbolic or rectified spirits would have been the preservatives which would suggest themselves to the medical mind, certainly not rough salt.'"

3. Holmes first realizes the identity of the person for whom the ears were intended when, Miss Cushing having insisted again that, "'I have not an enemy in the world,'" he notices something about her: "[H]e was staring with singular intentness at the lady's profile."

4. Holmes' case is complete when he learns two more things: firstly, that Miss Cushing's sister Sarah once lived with her other sister Mary and her husband Jim Browner, a seaman, but had quarrelled with them: "'Now she has no word hard enough for Jim Browner'"; and secondly, that Mary had lived briefly with Miss Cushing following this argument: "'[W]e kept on until about two months ago, when we had to part.'" At this point, Holmes knows the murderer and one of the victims.

Activity: For each of the clues write a clear account (on the activity sheet) about what Holmes was able to deduce and how it helped him to solve the mystery. To give you an idea, here is one done for you:

Clue #3.

Holmes first realizes the identity of the person for whom the ears were intended when, Miss Cushing having insisted again that, "'I have not an enemy in the world,'" he notices something about her: "[H]e was staring with singular intentness at the lady's profile."

Deduction: What Holmes notices when he looks at the profile of Miss Cushing is the similarity in structure between her ear and the female ear which was sent in the box. This makes it clear to Holmes that the female severed ear must belong to Miss Cushing's sister Mary, since the other sister, Sarah, is still alive.

Sherlock Holmes Short Stories by Sir Arthur Conan Doyle

Holmes and the Regular Police:

In this story the official police are represented by Inspector Lestrade of Scotland Yard. Lestrade is the most memorable of the detectives with whom Holmes works and appears in several of the stories. He seems to embody all of the faults (and a few of the qualities) of the regular police.

Activity: Answer these questions:

1. Look carefully at Lestrade's first letter to Holmes. *Find any* words or phrases in which Lestrade expresses confidence in being able to solve the mystery. Does the letter honestly represent Lestrade's feelings about the investigation?

2. What Holmes is trying to explain to Lestrade is the importance of the packaging in which the ears were sent. What do we learn of Lestrade from his two replies: "'I cannot see the importance,'" and, "'It is very neatly tied. I had already made a note to that effect,' said Lestrade complacently??

3. When Holmes announces his intention to ask Miss Cushing a few questions, Lestrade leaves saying: "'I think that I have nothing further to learn from Miss Cushing.'" What does this tell us of Lestrade?

4. Look carefully at Lestrade's second letter to Holmes. Why is Holmes so amused by Lestrade's use of the word 'we'? How does Holmes react to Lestrade's statement that: "'The affair proves, as I always though it would, to be an extremely simple one.'"?

5. What qualities does Lestrade have?

6. Holmes makes use of another policeman in his investigation. What is the man's name? Holmes refers to him as "'my friend.'" On the evidence of this story, why do you think that Holmes regards him so highly?

The Adventure of the Cardboard Box

Be a detective... "The Cardboard Box"

Activity: For each of the clues, write a clear account of what Holmes was able to deduce and how it helped him to solve the mystery.

Clue #1	The official police suspect a prank by some medical students. Holmes is quickly able to dismiss this possibility from his mind. He is able to deduce some things about the person who cut off the ears from details about the package in which the ears were sent. Although he draws these details to the attention of Inspector Lestrade, the Inspector fails to see their significance. Here are the points: "'It is a piece of tarred twine ... this knot is of a very peculiar character ... Brown paper, with a distinct smell of coffee.'"
Deduction	
Clue #2	Two other factors help him to disprove the medical student theory: "'They have been cut off with a blunt instrument ... carbolic or rectified spirits would have been the preservatives which would suggest themselves to the medical mind, certainly not rough salt.'"
Deduction	

Sherlock Holmes Short Stories by Sir Arthur Conan Doyle

Clue #3	Holmes first realizes the identity of the person for whom the ears were intended when, Miss Cushing having insistent again that, "'I have not an enemy in the world,'" he notices something about her: "[H]e was staring with singular intentness at the lady's profile."
Deduction	
Clue #4	Holmes' case is complete when he learns two more things: firstly, that Miss Cushing's sister Sarah once lived with her other sister Mary and her husband Jim Browner, a seaman, but had quarreled with them: "'Now she has no word hard enough for Jim Browner'"; and secondly, that Mary had lived briefly with Miss Cushing following this argument: "'[W]e kept on until about two months ago, when we had to part.'" At this point, Holmes knows the murderer and one of the victims.
Deduction	

The Adventure of the Cardboard Box

Plot Graph for the Sherlock Holmes Short Story:

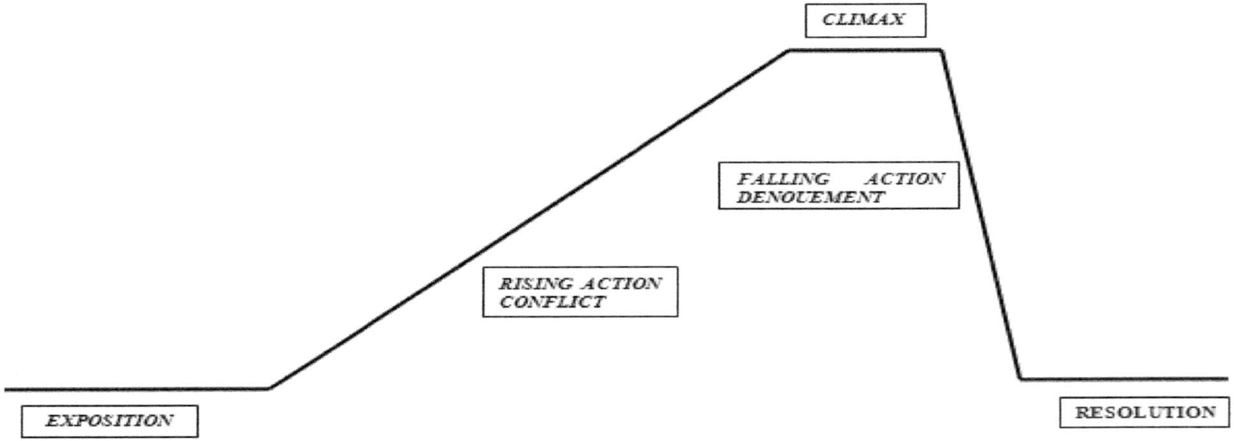

- EXPOSITION
- RISING ACTION / CONFLICT
- CLIMAX
- FALLING ACTION / DENOUEMENT
- RESOLUTION

Sherlock Holmes Short Stories by Sir Arthur Conan Doyle

The Final Problem

Introduction to "The Final Problem"

Sherlock Holmes proved to be very popular with the reading public with the result that Conan Doyle felt under a lot of pressure to keep writing Holmes stories. However, about the turn of the twentieth century, Doyle felt that he had written as much about Holmes as he wanted to, so he hit upon the simple idea of killing off the great detective. Although Holmes' body is never recovered, there is every reason to believe that Doyle (at least consciously) intended this to be the final appearance of the character. The result is a story which does not follow the usual pattern of Holmes narratives since it tells of the events leading to a crime rather than the investigation of a crime that has already happened. Later, of course, Conan Doyle bowed to the pressure of public opinion and brought his hero back from the grave, but that is another story (see "The Adventure of the Empty House" published in *The Strand Magazine*, October, 1903).

Structure of the Story:

The story falls into the following sections:
- Watson's explanation of why he has decided to write about the case;
- Watson explains how he became involved in the case;
- The statement of the story so far by Holmes;
- Holmes and Watson make their 'escape' from England;
- The final battle of wits between Holmes and Moriarty;
- Watson shows his powers of observation and deduction;
- Watson provides the sequel to the deaths of Holmes and Moriarty.

Activity: Locate in the text where each section begins and ends.

The Final Problem

The Detective's Methods:

There are no clues in this story, since there is no mystery to solve. Holmes appears deliberately to set himself up as a target for Moriarty as it becomes clearer and clearer to him that this is the only way to ensure the destruction of the evil criminal mastermind.

Activity: Answer these questions:
1. What is Holmes' motivation for wanting to destroy Moriarty?

2. What does this tell you about his attitude to crime at this point in his career?

Holmes and the Regular Police:

The regular police are important to the background of this story, though they do not actually appear.

Activity: Answer this question:

In what ways are the regular police useful to Holmes and why does he need to use them in this case?

Sherlock Holmes Short Stories by Sir Arthur Conan Doyle

Be a detective: The Death of Sherlock Holmes

Activity: Make a list of the evidence that leads Watson to conclude that Holmes dies with Moriarty at the Reichenbach Falls. Place your findings under two headings:

1. Proofs that Moriarty was determined to kill Holmes;

2. How the plan was carried out.

The Final Problem

1. Proofs that Moriarty was determined to kill Holmes

When it came to writing about the return of Sherlock Holmes, it was obviously neither possible nor necessary for Conan Doyle to change any of the details in this story that establish Moriarty's intention to kill Holmes. You should compare your gathering of this evidence with that below. Notice how there is a sense of inevitability about Holmes' 'death.' It is rather like a Greek or Shakespearean tragedy where the protagonist knows that his end is coming and accepts his fate.

1. Holmes knows himself to be a marked man. Following his interview with Professor Moriarty, there have been three attempts on his life in one day. His injured hand shows that he has had to fight for his life. Moriarty has threatened him with ""''inevitable destruction.''""

2. Holmes regards defeating Moriarty as the most important thing he can do, something for which he would be willing to die, ""'if I could beat that man, if I could free society of him, I should feel that my own career had reached its summit…'""

3. Moriarty tells Holmes that, ""''If you are clever enough to bring destruction upon me, rest assured that I shall do as much to you.''"" Holmes replies, effectively, that he would ""''cheerfully accept''"" death if it would ensure Moriarty's destruction.

4. Following the arrest by the police of his whole gang, Holmes tells Watson, ""'The man's occupation is gone… he will devote his whole energies to revenging himself on me.'""

5. When in Switzerland, Watson reports Holmes as repeatedly saying, that if he could be assured that society was freed from Professor Moriarty he would cheerfully bring his own career to a conclusion.

6. Whilst walking on a mountain path, a large boulder falls down the slope and nearly hits Holmes and the two men with him.

2. How the plan was carried out:

This is the part of the story on which Conan Doyle had to work. The evidence appears to be conclusive (except for the tantalizing lack of bodies), so he had to find an alternative interpretation of the 'facts,' for he needed a plausible scenario which would allow Holmes to have survived. The graphic below gives the 'facts' as Watson observed them and the interpretation he placed on them and leaves you to make notes on how Doyle might have revised and/or

Sherlock Holmes Short Stories by Sir Arthur Conan Doyle

reinterpreted them to explain Holmes' survival. (Clue: Watson applies the methods of Sherlock Holmes without having any aptitude for detection and so is prone to error.)

The 'facts' and Watson's conclusions	How the 'facts' can be reinterpreted to explain Holmes's survival.
At the Reichenbach Falls, Watson is separated from Holmes by a note which calls him back to his hotel to treat a dying lady. The note was written by Moriarty.	
On his way back to the hotel, Watson sees a "black figure" walking on the path leading to the falls. The man is Moriarty.	
Watson finds "Holmes's Alpine-stock (i.e., his walking stick) "leaning against the rock by which I had left him" near the end of the Path overlooking the falls. Clearly Holmes had not left the falls as he planned to.	
Of the "Swiss lad" who delivered the false message, there is no sign. Watson is sure that he was bribed by Moriarty.	
Watson observes in the soil of the path, "Two lines of footmarks ... There were none returning," and at the end of the path sees clear signs of struggle. The only conclusion seems to be that Moriarty followed Holmes to the end of the path and after a fight, both fell over the Falls	
Watson finds a note from Holmes apparently written just before the fatal conflict with Moriarty.	
At the end of the path Watson finds "the soil was all ploughed up into a patch of mud, and the brambles and ferns which fringed the chasm were torn and bedraggled." The inevitable conclusion is that "a personal contest between the two men ended... in their reeling over [the Falls], locked in each other's arms.	
Neither body is recovered due to "the dreadful cauldron of swirling water and seething foam" into which they fell.	

The Final Problem

Activity: Present your explanation of how Holmes escaped death. Below are two suggestions on how to do this, but feel free to come up with your own idea.

1. A timeline

The events of the fateful day (May 4th, 1891) when Holmes and Watson leave the Englischer Hof (let us say at 1 p.m.). Construct a timeline of events starting from that point and concluding with Watson finding and reading Holmes' note (let us say at 5 p.m.).

2. A narrative

In "The Empty House" Holmes has a lot of explaining to do! Watson, after getting over the initial shock of seeing his friend says, "'My dear chap, I am overjoyed to see you. Sit down and tell me how you came alive out of that dreadful chasm." It takes Holmes just over 1,000 words to explain what happened at the falls. You should be able to do it in about 500.
If you find it helpful, use this opening:
"As usual, my dear Watson, you observed accurately enough, but your conclusions were entirely wrong..."

Sherlock Holmes explains his escape to Dr. Watson

The following is Holmes' account of his encounter with Professor Moriarty at the Falls. It comes early in "The Empty Room" which is the first Holmes' short story to be published after Doyle gave way to public opinion (and the offer of a great deal of money) and brought back the great detective.

"My dear chap, I am overjoyed to see you. Sit down and tell me how you came alive out of that dreadful chasm." [Watson said]

"Well, then, about that chasm. I had no serious difficulty in getting out of it, for the very simple reason that I never was in it."

"You never were in it?"

"No, Watson, I never was in it. My note to you was absolutely genuine. I had little doubt that I had come to the end of my career when I perceived the somewhat sinister figure of the late Professor Moriarty standing upon the narrow pathway which led to safety. I read an inexorable purpose in his grey eyes. I exchanged some remarks with him, therefore, and obtained his courteous permission to write the short note which you afterwards received. I left it with my cigarette-box and my stick and I walked along the pathway, Moriarty still at my heels. When I reached the end I stood at bay. He drew no weapon, but he rushed at me and threw his long arms around me. He knew that his own game was up, and was only anxious to revenge himself upon me. We tottered together upon the brink of the fall. I have some knowledge, however, of baritsu, or the Japanese system of wrestling, which has more than once been very useful to me. I slipped through his grip, and he with a horrible scream kicked madly for a few seconds and clawed the air with both his hands. But for all his efforts he could not get his balance, and over he went. With my face over the brink I saw him fall for a long way. Then he struck a rock, bounded off, and splashed into the water."

I listened with amazement to this explanation, which Holmes delivered between the puffs of his cigarette.

"But the tracks!" I cried. "I saw with my own eyes that two went down the path and none returned."

"It came about in this way. The instant that the Professor had disappeared it struck me what a really extraordinarily lucky chance Fate had placed in my way. I knew that Moriarty was not the only man who had sworn my death. There were at least three others whose desire for vengeance upon me would only be increased by the death of their leader. They were all most dangerous men. One or other would certainly get me. On the other hand, if all the world was convinced that I was dead they would take liberties, these men, they would lay themselves open, and sooner or later I could destroy them. Then it would be time for me to announce that I was still in the land of the living. So rapidly does the brain act that I believe I had thought this all out before Professor Moriarty had reached the bottom of the Reichenbach Fall.

"I stood up and examined the rocky wall behind me. In your picturesque account of the matter, which I read with great interest some months later, you assert that the wall was sheer. This was not literally true. A few small footholds presented themselves, and there was some indication of a ledge. The cliff is so high that to climb it all was an obvious impossibility, and it was equally impossible to make my way along the wet path without leaving some tracks. I might, it is true, have reversed my boots, as I have done on similar occasions, but the sight of three sets of tracks in one direction would certainly have suggested a deception. On the whole, then, it was best that I should risk the climb. It was not a pleasant business, Watson. The fall roared beneath me. I am not a fanciful person, but I give you my word that I seemed to hear Moriarty's voice screaming at me out of the abyss. A mistake would have been fatal. More than once, as tufts of grass came out in my hand or my foot slipped in the wet notches of the rock, I thought that I was gone. But I struggled upwards, and at last I reached a ledge several feet deep and covered with soft green moss, where I could lie unseen in the most perfect comfort. There I was stretched when you, my dear Watson, and all your following were investigating in the most sympathetic and inefficient manner the circumstances of my death.

"At last, when you had all formed your inevitable and totally erroneous conclusions, you departed for the hotel and I was left alone. I had imagined that I had reached the end of my adventures, but a very unexpected

The Final Problem

occurrence showed me that there were surprises still in store for me. A huge rock, falling from above, boomed past me, struck the path, and bounded over into the chasm. For an instant I thought that it was an accident; but a moment later, looking up, I saw a man's head against the darkening sky, and another stone struck the very ledge upon which I was stretched, within a foot of my head. Of course, the meaning of this was obvious. Moriarty had not been alone. A confederate—and even that one glance had told me how dangerous a man that confederate was—had kept guard while the Professor had attacked me. From a distance, unseen by me, he had been a witness of his friend's death and of my escape. He had waited, and then, making his way round to the top of the cliff, he had endeavoured to succeed where his comrade had failed.

"I did not take long to think about it, Watson. Again I saw that grim face look over the cliff, and I knew that it was the precursor of another stone. I scrambled down on to the path. I don't think I could have done it in cold blood. It was a hundred times more difficult than getting up. But I had no time to think of the danger, for another stone sang past me as I hung by my hands from the edge of the ledge. Halfway down I slipped, but by the blessing of God I landed, torn and bleeding, upon the path. I took to my heels, did ten miles over the mountains in the darkness, and a week later I found myself in Florence with the certainty that no one in the world knew what had become of me."

Sherlock Holmes Short Stories by Sir Arthur Conan Doyle

Plot Graph for the Sherlock Holmes Short Story:

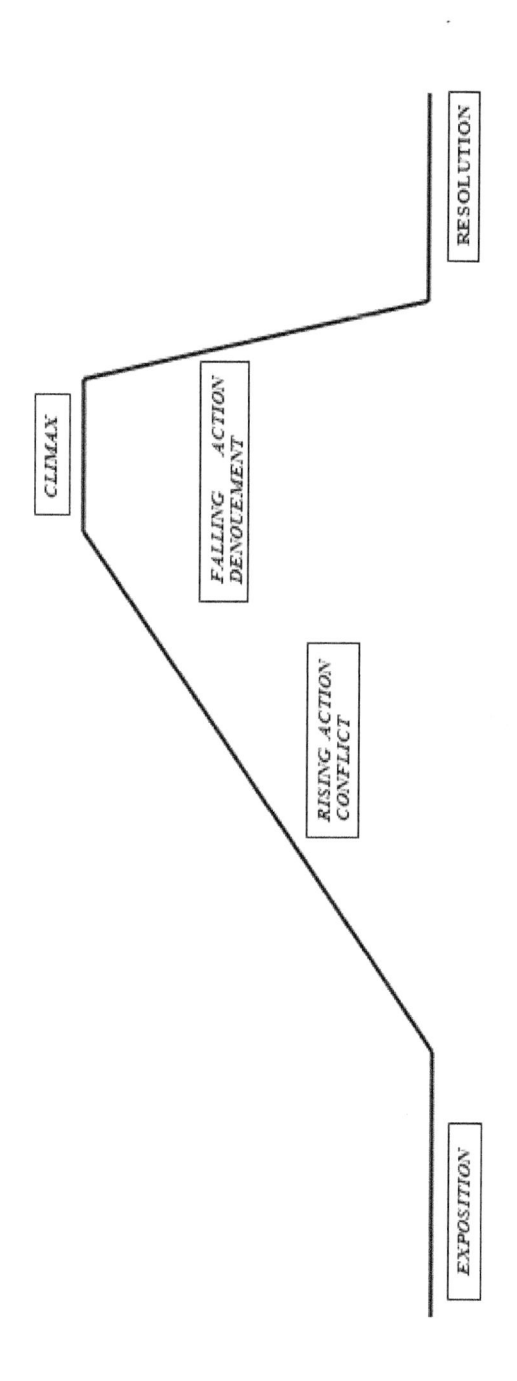

- EXPOSITION
- RISING ACTION / CONFLICT
- CLIMAX
- FALLING ACTION / DENOUEMENT
- RESOLUTION

Reading Group Use of the Study Guide Questions

Although there are both closed and open questions in the Study Guide, very few of them have simple, right or wrong answers. They are designed to encourage in-depth discussion, disagreement, and (eventually) consensus. Above all, they aim to encourage readers to go to the text to support their conclusions and interpretations.

I am not so arrogant as to presume to tell readers how they should use this resource. I used it in the following ways, each of which ensured that group members were well prepared for group discussion and presentations.

1. Set a reading assignment for the group and tell everyone to be aware that the questions will be the focus of whole group discussion at the next meeting.

2. Set a reading assignment for the group and allocate particular questions to sections of the group (e.g. if there are four questions, divide the group into four sections, etc.).

In the meeting, form discussion groups containing one person who has prepared each question and allow time for feedback within the groups.

Have feedback to the whole the on each question by picking a group at random to present their answers and to follow up with a group discussion.

3. Set a reading assignment for the group, but do not allocate questions.

In the meeting, divide readers into groups and allocate to each group one of the questions related to the reading assignment, the answer to which they will have to present formally to the meeting.

Allow time for discussion and preparation.

4. Set a reading assignment for the group, but do not allocate questions.

In the meeting, divide readers into groups and allocate to each group one of the questions related to the reading assignment.

Allow time for discussion and preparation.

Now reconfigure the groups so that each group contains at least one person who has prepared each question and allow time for feedback within the groups.

5. Before starting to read the text, allocate specific questions to individuals or pairs. (It is best not to allocate all questions to allow for other approaches and variety. One in three questions or one in four seems about right.) Tell readers that they will be leading the group discussion on their question. They will need to start with a brief presentation of the issues and then conduct a question and answer session. After this, they will be expected to present a

Sherlock Holmes Short Stories by Sir Arthur Conan Doyle

brief review of the discussion.

6. Having finished the text, arrange the meeting into groups of 3, 4 or 5. Tell each group to select as many questions from the Study Guide as there are members of the group.

Each individual is responsible for drafting out an answer to one question, and each answer should be substantial.

Each group as a whole is then responsible for discussing, editing and suggesting improvements to each answer.

The Reverend Lyle Thorne Mysteries

If you enjoy detective short stories, you will love my series featuring policeman turned vicar Lyle Thorne (1860-1947)

Investigations of The Reverend Lyle Thorne (Volume One)
Thorne investigates five cases spanning the years 1911-1927:
- The fallen woman loses more than her life...
- The anonymous cleric pleads for a murder suspect...
- The Italian bride is frightened by mysterious disappearances...
- The missing betrothed vanishes the day before her wedding...
- A hanged man is still swinging in a locked room...

Further Investigations of The Reverend Lyle Thorne (Volume Two)
Thorne investigates five cases spanning the years 1910-1912:
- The wedding of an American heiress and divorcee is cancelled by the inexplicable disappearance of her ring...
- An Oxford antiquarian is found lying on a hoard of medieval coins...
- The young bride-to-be of a rich widower receives frightening threats...
- A Sussex landowner walks calmly into the courtyard of his house and vanishes...
- Thorne must find a husband who has taken great care not to be found...

Early Investigations of Lyle Thorne (Volume Three)
Thorne investigates five cases spanning the years 1876 to 1889:
- In Thorne's first ever investigation, his father is accused of murder by a dead man...
- Having been told to meet his step-father at 1 p.m., a young boy sets off from home at 12.45 p.m. and is never seen alive again...
- Twins plan and execute a perfect murder...
- A baby disappears from the nursery of the London home of the Duke and Duchess of Albermarle...
- Thorne's investigations put a name to Jack the Ripper but at terrible personal cost...
- Sanditon Investigations of The Rev. Lyle **Thorne (Volume Four)**

Thorne investigates five cases spanning the years 1912-1914:
- A young girl disappears for the second time, this time from an enclosed garden...
- A modern painter dies of a heart attack – a natural death until the coffin falls and breaks open at the burial...
- A bishop in line to become Archbishop of Canterbury is poisoned in

his own library...
- Thorne's curate encounters a young girl abandoned on the promenade...
- The discovery of the body of a man stabbed to death more than two centuries ago sets Thorne the ultimate investigative challenge...

Final Investigations of The Rev. Lyle Thorne (Volume Five)
Thorne investigates five cases spanning the years 1927-1948:
- A photographer's kiosk is burned down on the same day as Sanditon's biggest jewel robbery...
- A school master is found poisoned a few days before his retirement...
- A shell-shocked soldier becomes obsessed by "the lady in the dark"...
- A young railway worker implicated in a robbery is found murdered...
- Thorne witnesses the discovery of an 'impossible' murder-robbery at a bank in Sanditon...

Lost Investigation of The Rev. Lyle Thorne (Volume Six)
Thorne investigates five cases spanning the years 1908 - 1912:
- A runner is seen entering the tunnel under a railway line and is never seen again...
- Rev. Thorne's curate is accused of the theft of a valuable sapphire pendant from a dying woman...
- The body of a local man is washed up on Sanditon beach, but his empty cottage is found to be locked from the inside...
- The abrupt dismissal of a scullery maid alerts Thorne to two crimes...
- A mysterious and glamorous American widow is abducted, and the body of her abductor is found the next day...

Official Investigations of Lyle Thorne (Volume Seven)
As a young member of the Metropolitan Police, Thorne investigates five cases spanning the years 1881 – 1887:
- An apparently simple case of murder reveals Thorne's ability to see beyond the obvious...
- Three young women plan a holiday excursion to Margate, but events take a tragic turn...
- Thorne realizes that an innocent man will be hung and that it is his evidence that has convicted him...
- A weekly tea party leaves one woman dead and another in the hospital...
- An international criminal wagers the Commissioner of Police that he can commit the perfect crime...

Clerical Investigations of The Rev. Lyle Thorne (Volume Eight)
As a newly ordained minister in the Church of England, Thorne investigates three cases spanning the years 1896 – 1898:
- A curate inexplicably leaves his parish in the middle of the night, just as two years earlier the former vicar had also left…
- A vicar in Leeds is found kneeling over the dead body of his wife with the murder weapon in his hand…
- The manuscript of an ancient Lindisfarne gospel and its modern translation disappear from a locked strongbox, in a locked desk, in a locked room…

About the Author

Ray Moore was born in Nottingham, England. He obtained his Master's Degree in Literature from Lancaster University and taught in secondary education for twenty-eight years before relocating to Florida with his wife. There he taught English and Information Technology in the International Baccalaureate Program. He is now a full-time writer and fitness fanatic and leads a reading group at a local library.

Website: http://www.raymooreauthor.com

Ray strives to make his texts the best that they can be. If you have any comments or question about this book *please* contact the author through his email:

villageswriter@gmail.com

Also by Ray Moore:

Books are available from amazon.com and from barnesandnoble.com as paperbacks and some from online eBook retailers.

Fiction:

The Lyle Thorne Mysteries Volumes One to Eight. (as detailed previously)

Non-fiction:

The ***Critical Introduction series*** is written for high school teachers and students and for college undergraduates. Each volume gives an in-depth analysis of a key text:

"The Stranger" by Albert Camus: A Critical Introduction (Revised Second Edition)
"The General Prologue" by Geoffrey Chaucer: A Critical Introduction
"Pride and Prejudice" by Jane Austen: A Critical Introduction
"The Great Gatsby" by F. Scott Fitzgerald: A Critical Introduction

The Text and Critical Introduction series differs from the Critical introduction series as these books contain the original text and in the case of the medieval texts an interlinear translation to aid the understanding of the text. The commentary allows the reader to develop a deeper understanding of the text and themes within the text.

"Sir Gawain and the Green Knight": Text and Critical Introduction*
"The General Prologue" by Geoffrey Chaucer: Text and Critical Introduction*
"Heart of Darkness" by Joseph Conrad: Text and Critical Introduction*
"Henry V" by William Shakespeare: Text and Critical Introduction*
"Oedipus Rex" by Sophocles: Text and Critical Introduction*
"A Room with a View" By E.M. Forster: Text and Critical Introduction*
"The Sign of Four" by Sir Arthur Conan Doyle Text and Critical Introduction

"The Wife of Bath's Prologue and Tale" by Geoffrey Chaucer: Text and Critical Introduction*
Jane Austen: The Complete Juvenilia: Text and Critical Introduction

Study Guides - listed alphabetically by author

Study Guides offer an in-depth look at aspects of a text. They generally include an introduction to the characters, genre, themes, setting, tone of a text. They also may include activities on helpful literary terms as well as graphic organizers to aid understanding of the plot and different perspectives of characters.

* denotes also available as an eBook

"ME and EARL and the Dying GIRL" by Jesse Andrews: A Study Guide
Study Guide to "Alias Grace" by Margaret Atwood*
Study Guide to "The Handmaid's Tale" by Margaret Atwood*
"Pride and Prejudice" by Jane Austen: A Study Guide
"Moloka'i" by Alan Brennert: A Study Guide
"Wuthering Heights" by Emily Brontë: A Study Guide *
Study Guide on "Jane Eyre" by Charlotte Brontë*
"The Myth of Sisyphus" by Albert Camus: A Study Guide
"The Stranger" by Albert Camus: A Study Guide
"The Myth of Sisyphus" and "The Stranger" by Albert Camus: Two Study Guides *
Study Guide to "Death Comes to the Archbishop" by Willa Cather
"The Awakening" by Kate Chopin: A Study Guide
Study Guide to Seven Short Stories by Kate Chopin
Study Guide to "Ready Player One" by Ernest Cline
Study Guide to "Disgrace" by J. M. Coetzee
"The Meursault Investigation" by Kamel Daoud: A Study Guide
Study Guide on "Great Expectations" by Charles Dickens*
"The Sign of Four" by Sir Arthur Conan Doyle: A Study Guide *
Study Guide to "Manhattan Beach" by Jennifer Egan
"The Wasteland, Prufrock and Poems" by T.S. Eliot: A Study Guide
Study Guide on "Birdsong" by Sebastian Faulks*
"The Great Gatsby" by F. Scott Fitzgerald: A Study Guide
"A Room with a View" by E. M. Forster: A Study Guide
"Looking for Alaska" by John Green: A Study Guide
"Paper Towns" by John Green: A Study Guide
Study Guide to "Turtles All the Way Down" by John Green
Study Guide to "Florida" by Lauren Groff
Study Guide on "Catch-22" by Joseph Heller *
"Unbroken" by Laura Hillenbrand: A Study Guide
"The Kite Runner" by Khaled Hosseini: A Study Guide
"A Thousand Splendid Suns" by Khaled Hosseini: A Study Guide

Sherlock Holmes Short Stories by Sir Arthur Conan Doyle
"The Secret Life of Bees" by Sue Monk Kidd: A Study Guide
Study Guide on "The Invention of Wings" by Sue Monk Kidd
Study Guide to "Fear and Trembling" by Søren Kierkegaard
"Go Set a Watchman" by Harper Lee: A Study Guide
Study Guide to "Pachinko" by Min Jin Lee
"On the Road" by Jack Keruoac: A Study Guide
Study Guide on "Life of Pi" by Yann Martel*
Study Guide to "Death of a Salesman" by Arthur Miller
Study Guide to "The Bluest Eye" by Toni Morrison
Study Guide to "Reading Lolita in Tehran" by Azir Nafisi
Study Guide to "The Sympathizer" by Viet Thanh Nguyen
"Animal Farm" by George Orwell: A Study Guide
Study Guide on "Nineteen Eighty-Four" by George Orwell
Study Guide to "The Essex Serpent" by Sarah Perry
Study Guide to "Selected Poems" and Additional Poems by Sylvia Plath*
"An Inspector Calls" by J.B. Priestley: A Study Guide
Study Guide to "Cross Creek" by Marjorie Kinnan Rawlings
"Esperanza Rising" by Pam Munoz Ryan: A Study Guide
Study Guide to "The Catcher in the Rye" by J.D. Salinger
"Where'd You Go, Bernadette" by Maria Semple: A Study Guide
"Henry V" by William Shakespeare: A Study Guide
Study Guide on "Macbeth" by William Shakespeare *
"Othello" by William Shakespeare: A Study Guide *
Study Guide on "Antigone" by Sophocles*
"Oedipus Rex" by Sophocles: A Study Guide
"Cannery Row" by John Steinbeck: A Study Guide
"East of Eden" by John Steinbeck: A Study Guide
"The Grapes of Wrath" by John Steinbeck: A Study Guide
"Of Mice and Men" by John Steinbeck: A Study Guide*
"The Goldfinch" by Donna Tartt: A Study Guide
Study Guide to "The Hate U Give" by Angie Thomas
"Walden; or, Life in the Woods" by Henry David Thoreau: A Study Guide
Study Guide to "Cat's Cradle" by Kurt Vonnegut
"The Bridge of San Luis Rey" by Thornton Wilder: A Study Guide *
Study Guide on "The Book Thief" by Markus Zusak

Study Guides available only as e-books:
Study Guide on "Cross Creek" by Marjorie Kinnan Rawlings.
Study Guide on "Heart of Darkness" by Joseph Conrad:
Study Guide on "The Mill on the Floss" by George Eliot
Study Guide on "Lord of the Flies" by William Golding
Study Guide on "Nineteen Eighty-Four" by George Orwell

Study Guide on "Henry IV Part 2" by William Shakespeare
Study Guide on "Julius Caesar" by William Shakespeare
Study Guide on "The Pearl" by John Steinbeck
Study Guide on "Slaughterhouse-Five" by Kurt Vonnegut

New titles are added regularly.

Readers' Guides

Readers' Guides offer an introduction to important aspects of the text and questions for personal reflection and/or discussion. Guides are written for individual readers who wish to explore texts in depth and for members of Reading Circles who wish to make their discussions of texts more productive.

A Reader's Guide to Becoming by Michelle Obama
A Reader's Guide to Educated: A Memoir by Tara Westover

Teacher resources: Ray also publishes many more study guides and other resources for classroom use on the 'Teachers Pay Teachers' website: **http://www.teacherspayteachers.com/Store/Raymond-Moore**

Printed in Great Britain
by Amazon